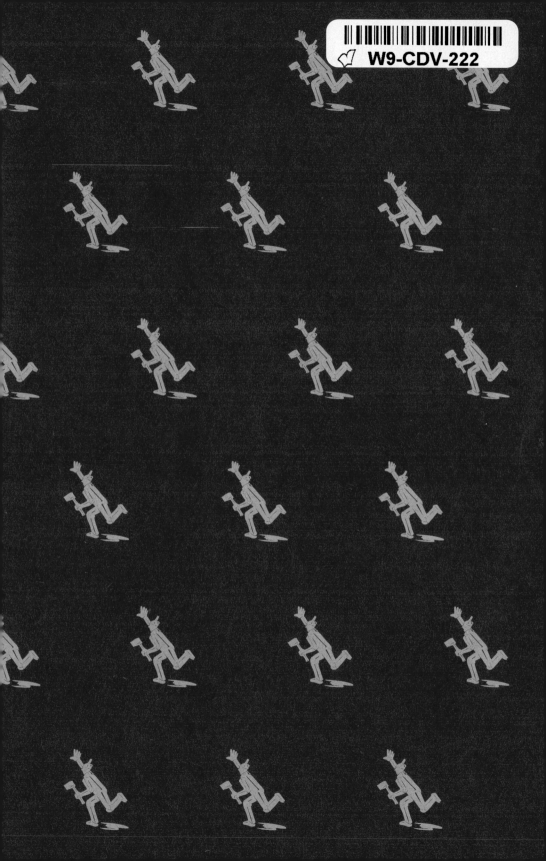

The Other Side of Oz

by
BUDDY EBSEN

edited by
Stephen Cox

DONOVAN
PUBLISHING

Newport Beach, California
1993

Publisher's Cataloging in Publication
(Prepared by Quality Books Inc.)

Ebsen, Buddy, 1908-
   The other side of Oz / by Buddy Ebsen.
   p. cm.
   Includes bibliographical references.
   LCCN: 93-073697
   ISBN: 1-8805838-08-3

   1. Ebsen, Buddy, 1908-   2. Television actors and actresses--United States--Biography. 3. Motion picture actors and actresses--United States--Biography. I. Title.

PN1992.4.E37E37 1993   791.45'092
                                      QBI93-21681

First Edition
Printed in the United States of America
10 9 8 7 6 5 4 3 2 1

2808 LAFAYETTE AVENUE
NEWPORT BEACH, CA 92663 USA
"The Books That Matter"™

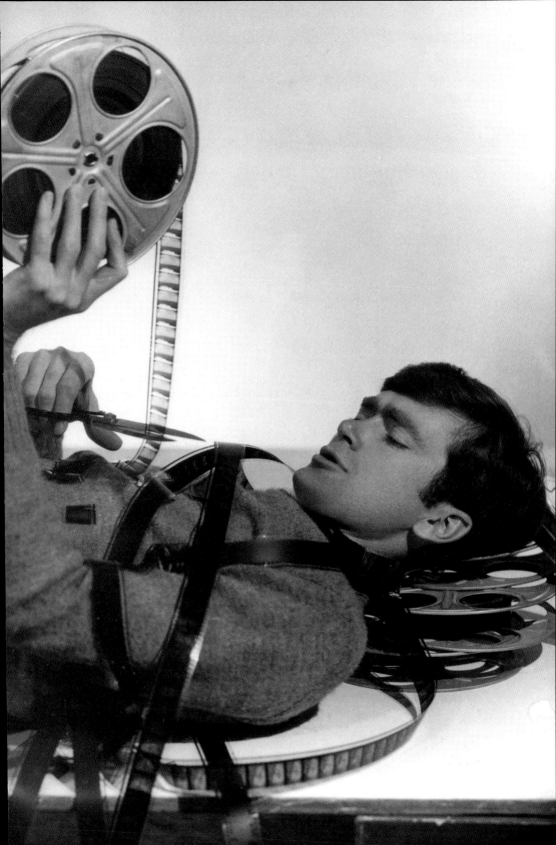

DEDICATION

This book is dedicated to

my Father and Mother,

Christian and Frances Ebsen,

who throughout their lives gave

a thousandfold more than they took.

CONTENTS

MY WIFE DOROTHY AND ME WITH BOB HOPE AT "THE FRIENDS OF CHILDHELP" GALA
HONORING GINGER ROGERS, MAY 13, 1991.

FOREWORD

Buddy has penned an absolutely delightful entertainment autobiography about his classic career that encompasses the Broadway stage, the silver screen, and television. By longevity alone, he is more qualified than anyone else to provide the world with an overview of the flip side of show business.

His career is one of the most successful and colorful in the industry. Legendary? Yes! Hey, not many people give up pre-med for tap dancing or get a job in a Broadway musical the first day they arrive in New York City. (True, he lost that job six days later because he was too tall.) His mentors were vaudevillians; his inspiration was his sister and dancing partner, Vilma; and among his fans were Al Capone and Noel Coward.

Buddy's story has appeal for young and old: from his life-threatening experiences on the original set of *The Wizard of Oz* to service at sea in World War II; from the blazing saga of Disney's *Davy Crockett* and the poignant *Breakfast At Tiffany's* to the all-American favorites "The Beverly Hillbillies" and "Barnaby Jones"—and more recently—a return to the stage at The Roy Clark Celebrity Theatre in Branson, Missouri.

What is remarkable about Buddy's book is that he provides a profound journal of the "Other Side" of show business without displacing the glitter that makes Hollywood special. Special, not only to the fans—but to those of us who continue looking, always hoping, to find what's over that rainbow.

Bob Hope

ACKNOWLEDGMENTS

To reiterate a well known—but too often unexpressed—fact: You can accomplish nothing in this world without help. And so it is with this book.

To the many friends, co-workers, and generous folks of goodwill whose contributions have made my book a reality, I extend my deepest heartfelt gratitude.

First, I want to thank my beautiful wife Dorothy, then my contributing editor Stephen Cox, along with: Ken Allison, Jacque Anderson, Max Baer, Jr., Chuck Bailey, Ken Beck, Dave Black, Eric Daily, Gilda Davis, Rick deLome, Win Fiandaca, Bert Fink, William Hammerstein, Paul Henning, Ellen Kasemeier, Mark Patterson, George Posanke, Gabi Rona, Joan Runkel, Ken Ross, Paul Sumner, Shirley Temple, Teressa Tucker, Ted Turner and Phyllis J. Wilce.

Bob Hope loves America—every acre of it. In the 1950s he decided to buy up the Santa Monica Mountains.

Somehow—through what must have been a slip-up by his business affairs people—I was able to squirrel off a little thirty-five acre chunk from the heart of his heartland to create a horse ranch for my horse-crazy kids.

Being the big man that he is, Bob gave it no more than a gnat's notice—if he was even aware of it.

Ten years later, when the "Hillbillies" hit, Bob asked

me how much money I'd want to appear on his variety show.

When I said, "Well, neighbor—no money," his eyes widened, "but you know that little three-acre piece of yours that adjoins my land, just this side of the gully? For the deed to that land, I'd do your show—twice!"

Bob looked at me with new respect—grinned—patted me on the head and changed the subject.

And that, regretfully, is as close as I ever came to working with this beloved and universally acclaimed national treasure.

When my publisher asked me whom I'd prefer to write the foreword to this book, I could think of only one person: someone of my own vintage and with a similar background, someone who spoke and understood the same language and whose attitude is flavored with humor— another hoofer. Bob Hope.

But would he do it? All you can do is ask. But would it be given? It was!

So, to Bob and Dolores, that ideal loving couple, my eternal thanks.

Buddy Ebsen

INTRODUCTION

The "Land of Oz" has just one Wizard. The realm of "show business" has many. They range from Ziegfeld, Hammerstein, Griffith, De Mille and Disney in the past—to Spielberg, Lucas, Cameron, Ron Howard and that myriad of other young, budding Wizards whose numbers compound daily. And as the reigning powers in Hollywood—our modern Land of Oz—they relentlessly drive themselves to outdo each other as they create that glittering, captivating magic called entertainment.

Audiences see this realm from one aspect. Here's how it looks from the other side.

"Money is no object," said Mr. Mayer. "But in order to give you the kind of parts you deserve, Ebsen, we have to own you."

There was something about the word "own" and the way Louis B. Mayer said it that sent a grating, chilling shock through me, like when you suddenly ground your keel on a rock. I was currently being paid $1,500 a week in a complicated and unheard-of two-year motion picture contract. "Money is no object" usually meant a possible $1,000 bonus just to sign. With options and raises over the standard seven-year contract, the offer could go to five thousand, which was the absolute top salary of any of the MGM stars: Gable, Shearer, Crawford, Beery, the entire stable—all "owned."

Of course, in 1939, $5,000 bought what twenty-five thousand would buy today, and there were no multimillion-dollar film actors like Stallone, Hoffman, Redford and Costner. For starring in that super blockbusting classic *Gone With the Wind*, which premiered in Atlanta, December 4, 1939, Clark Gable received only his regular salary, minus a loan-out bonus, which was sometimes granted by a generous studio boss.

The structural facts supporting the Gable deal, as recorded by Hollywood historians, establish Mayer as the absolute and merciless King of the Jungle in the high-stakes monopoly game moviemakers played with real money.

David O. Selznick, who had bought the film rights of the Margaret Mitchell novel *Gone With the Wind* for $50,000, unwittingly trapped himself downstream, by inviting the public to influence the casting of the picture.

Fourteen hundred unknowns and half the actresses in Hollywood were tested for the role of Scarlett O'Hara, but with one voice the public demanded Gable to play Rhett. To get Gable, Selznick was forced to give up the film's juicy dis-

tribution rights and half its profits to Gable's "owner"—
Selznick's father-in-law—L.B. Mayer.

In those days, Hollywood was a company town controlled by six or seven bosses of major film companies, and
two of those were interlocked through the Schenk family.
Nicholas Schenk controlled Loews Incorporated, which controlled Metro-Goldwyn-Mayer; his brother, Joe, controlled
Twentieth Century-Fox. All the companies were cutthroat
competitors in the market but were quick to close ranks
when an actor showed signs of rebellion, or just a hint of
that taboo word: "independence." Deals and amounts paid
to actors were often arrived at casually, but carefully, in
small talk over the Saturday night poker table located in
Louis B. Mayer's Santa Monica beach house.

And there I was in 1939, looking across a large polished desk at the acknowledged most powerful of the powerful in a super-powerful business; he was the reigning
Wizard in this Land of Oz. Mayer wasn't really a bad man.
Just had to own people. That's the way it was.

"Mr. Mayer," I said (and now, viewed through my
years of accumulated wisdom and maturity, I often wonder
where this muley kid found these words and the gall to say
them), "Mr. Mayer, here's the kind of fool I am. You can't
own me. I can't be a piece of goods on your counter."

Sometime later, back in vaudeville, my sister Vilma
and I were working for a fraction of the money I had turned
down in California. It was late one February night, and we
were driving across the Poconos in Pennsylvania on our
way to New York to catch an 8:00 A.M. train for Toronto the
next day. Around us swirled a sleet and ice storm of historic
proportions. Sleet was freezing on the limbs of trees and

electric transmission lines until the weight of the ice broke them, and they fell across the road adding perils to our travel. Ice was forming on our windshield. We had no heater because my friend George L. George had insisted, "Don't get a heater for the car. I'll get you one wholesale." (He did, the following July.)

I had to drive with my window open, leaning out taking the sleet on my eyeballs, in order to see past the blinding headlights of coal trucks in the approaching lane. Once in a while I stopped and tried to scrape the ice off the windshield with a pocket comb. Vilma huddled in the passenger seat, wrapping herself in her costume to keep warm. Suddenly I began to laugh so loudly, so uproariously and so long that she said to me, "What-in-the-hell can you find to laugh about at a time like this?"

My answer was wry but exultant, free, born of high comedy, as triumphantly viewed from a personal mountain peak.

"L.B. Mayer ain't tellin' *me* what to do."

There are just three times in my life when I actually thought I was going to die. The first was back in Belleville, Illinois, at age ten, while taking a short cut home across a hundred-yard-long railroad trestle. Halfway across, the train made its appearance, bursting without warning from around the bend; it was coming at me full-bore.

It was a fifty-foot drop to the rocks below, but less near the train. I made a snap decision and sprinted over the widely spaced railroad ties straight toward this smoke-belching behemoth barreling at me. At the fifteen-foot-drop level, I launched. A bush broke my fall, reducing my injuries to two sprained ankles and a lot of scratches.

I never told my mother how I got them.

The second time was while driving home from the Disney Studios, where I was filming a motion picture. I fell asleep on the freeway and hit an overpass abutment. Fortunately I was driving a half-ton pickup, so when my left front fender made glancing contact with the steel-reinforced concrete of the overpass, instead of flipping, my vehicle merely made a slithering 180-degree change of heading and stopped. Now the unfortunate part of the story begins.

Naturally, the jolt woke me up. I was sitting in the center lane of the southbound 605 Freeway—facing north. The blinding headlights of the peak Friday-night traffic were coming toward me at a minimum of sixty-five miles per hour.

My headlights were still on, but unfortunately the shock of impact had disturbed the flow of gas to the carburetor. My engine was as dead as I was going to be in seconds.

From somewhere I found the "cool" to activate the ignition switch. Once—nothing. Twice—nothing. The third time—with a prayer—a sputtering start—then a roar. I still had a chance—and a problem: I'm stalled fifty feet onto the overpass where there is no road shoulder, and I have to drive that distance into this oncoming phalanx of traffic just to get off the road.

The car-swerving, tire-shrieking sounds generated by that fifty-foot drive which seemed to last forever, as aston-

ished and outraged drivers fought to avoid the headlights coming straight at them from the wrong direction, will be forever with me.

Why did God's third "near miss" occur during the making of *The (Wonderful) Wizard of Oz*, for me not so wonderful? What was he saving me for?

Ah, sweet mystery of life—and, of course, that *other* condition.

In spite of subsequent events—and their murky memories—who would have bet that one day I would marry a lovely girl named Dorothy and live just around the corner from a street actually named "The Yellow Brick Road?"

Of all the questions asked of me in recent years, two of the most frequent are: "How old was Granny?" and "Is it true you were the original Tin Man in *The Wizard of Oz*?"

The answer to the first is, "I never had the guts to ask her," and to the second—well—

"Come and listen to my story. . . ."

THE BEGINNING

Other than my seven lean years (1947 through 1953), I have enjoyed an almost unbroken series of successes in show business. Since 1962, after the birth of "The Beverly Hillbillies" through 1972, followed by eight years with "Barnaby Jones," I have been blessed with a solid continuity of employment in a dislocated industry notorious for its lack of security. Perhaps a hundred interviewers and many baffled actors have asked me point-blank how I managed to survive. When I look at myself on the screen, I ask the same question. I am certainly not—and never have been—the world's greatest actor, the world's greatest dancer, and most assuredly not the world's greatest singer. Often I would parry the questions with a flip, "I do a magic act," or "when I get up to bat I try to pick a good one, swing from the heels

I WAS AN ALL-AMERICAN BOY. 1920

and pray." I did a lot of praying during my seven lean years. And I never left a dressing room without thanking God for the job.

Vaudevillian Bert Wheeler, formerly of the team Wheeler and Woolsey who were featured comedians in Ziegfeld musicals, once told me that in the old days—1915 to 1925—an act could play for three years in the New York area without changing hotel rooms. During that time, if they prudently fed the "grouch bag" (saved and lived modestly), they might have the down payment on that little chicken farm in Jersey that all sensible vaudeville acts hoped to retire to one day. Then came radio, and many of these acts made the transition—big. Ex-vaudevillians Eddie Cantor, Jack Benny, Burns and Allen, Ed Wynn, Jack Pearl, Fred Allen, the Easy Aces, Fibber McGee and Molly, and later Bob Hope could have all retired to peacock farms with their fabulous earnings in radio.

But while some prospered in this new mechanical show business, others just didn't fit in. It was great for talking and singing acts whose material could be readily replenished by a staff of writers, but some great acts like Herb Williams, Smith and Dale, Professor Lamberti, and Willie West and McGinty had to wait until the Ed Sullivan/Milton Berle era of television. And then, their beautifully organized mosaics of comedy bits—which had been carefully collected and perfectly honed over the years—were used up in one performance on television.

Show business, taken over by the agencies and the networks, became a free medicine show. As the box office disappeared, so did the theater and the three years of playing time around New York that Bert Wheeler had spoken of.

And so the great acts, which couldn't make it in this new medicine show, retired to their chicken farms or just drifted into obscurity. (Unless Neil Simon happened to write a play about them.)

We entered an era where just a handful of performers entertained the nation each night for free in their living rooms, and thousands of talented, skilled, worthwhile and hardworking people went jobless.

When I think over sixty years, through all the phases of show business I have experienced and survived—including musical comedy, vaudeville, night clubs, the legitimate theater, motion pictures and television—there is no question that television has provided my most material success and though currently receiving sharp criticism from many angles—some with cause—how could I be other than grateful to the medium? As far as I am concerned, television was invented to sell Buddy Ebsen.

Writing such a book as this calls for rigid self-examination. It's easy enough to tell *how* I survived. But *why* is something else. To search for those clues I have to go back more than sixty years. More like eighty.

I was born in Belleville, Illinois, at four o'clock in the morning on April 2, 1908. The people of Belleville were mostly of German extraction, and the economics of the little town rested primarily upon the harvests from the rich farmland surrounding it. There were also coal mines, a foundry and stoneworks, and a brewery. Later, during World War I, the establishment of Scott Field Air Base four miles away supplemented the town's cash flow and gave it economic stability. Three railroads ran through town, and a streetcar line carried people to St. Louis fourteen miles away.

St. Louis, known to our family as "The City," was an important place in my world from an early date; that's where the chocolate came from. Huge freeform chunks of it were broken from gigantic cakes and brought to us by my aunt, *Tante* Marie, upon returning from her bimonthly shopping trips to The City. The candy came from the "Busy Bee Candy Store," which I easily identified by their flying bee logo on her net shopping bag, long before I could read.

My father was born at Neibel in Denmark, near Flensburg on the German border. Like most border countries, the land has changed sovereignty so many times that the people of that region are neither typically Danish nor typically German. They are Schleswig-Holsteiners and seem more friendly, more buoyant of spirit, and more optimistic than the stolid Germans and the "iron hatted" Danes.

My father came to this land of opportunity at sixteen, partly because during one of Bismarck's realignments of the German-Danish border, his older brothers found themselves dragooned into the German army. Their horror stories of German army discipline persuaded my father to book passage on the first available ship for America. He arrived in Chicago in the late 1890s, and found a natural base in the home of his older sister Alvina, who was comfortably established as the wife of the postmaster of that city.

Being athletic, he gravitated toward *Turnvereins*. These were German-American athletic and social clubs which stressed gymnastics, field, and track events and beer garden *gemütlichkeit* (warm friendliness!). The *Turnverein* had a normal school in Indianapolis, which trained instructors who were then assigned, as positions became available, to *Turnvereins* in various towns and cities throughout the Middle West. After floating around Chicago and working at various jobs for several years, my father chose his profession. He enrolled in the normal school and upon graduation attained a post at a *Turnverein* in the little German town of Belleville, Illinois.

In spite of the natural interest undoubtedly shown by the crop of young females toward a new man in town, my father, when loneliness overtook him, could not forget a spunky eighteen-year old he had met while skating in Milwaukee. And so he sent for the girl who became my

MY MOTHER, FRANCES EBSEN. 1978

mother, and they were married by a Justice of the Peace at the Belleville House just north of the town square. They settled down in one room at the boarding house nearby, and that is how my four sisters and I came to be born in Belleville, Illinois.

As I have said, my father, Christian Ebsen, was an optimistic man. He was also enterprising, progressive, had a great deal of charm, and had a strong need to be surrounded by open space. Entering into the beer garden sociability of the little community, he made friends easily. One of these friends was Colonel Andle who was the prominent and respected head of one of the old families of Belleville. He was a colonel by virtue of having commanded a regiment in the Civil War.

Having discovered nine acres of land on the outskirts

of town that suited his purpose, my father immediately began persuading Colonel Andle to loan him the money to buy it. Once the land was in Dad's possession, he promptly built a small shack on a hill, which became the first Ebsen home; then he dammed up a group of springs which surfaced on the property. The resulting pond became the Ebsen Natatorium and in no time at all my father was engaged in teaching most of the inhabitants of St. Clair County how to swim.

I learned to swim almost as soon as I learned to walk. By age four I roamed the place at will, shooting at blue jays and bullfrogs with homemade bows and arrows and voyaging across the pond on a discarded oak diving board. One day I discovered that by standing on the board and holding a towel in a certain way the wind would carry me across the water. It was the same discovery that primitive peoples must have made when they stood up in their log canoes to stretch, and felt their furs catch the wind. This was a pleasurable first sailing experience for me, a discovery that would deeply influence my entire life.

The years in Belleville flew by. They were happy years. The Ebsen family grew to seven—actually eight, counting *Tante* Marie, my mother's sister who came from Milwaukee to help raise us five kids. There were four girls— Helga, Norma, Vilma, Leslie—and me. I was in the middle. It has been said that surrounded by six females, I must've been spoiled and waited on hand and foot. I don't see—or remember—it that way.

In the summer, we all pitched in and helped with the Ebsen Natatorium and picnic grounds. I was a locker boy and later an apprentice lifeguard. As the fame of the place

EBSEN'S NATATORIUM

A Popular High-Class Pleasure Resort

The population of Belleville being mostly Germans and descendants of the German pioneers who left their homes in Germany for a land of more freedom and more opportunity, it quite naturally follows that Belleville is also a city where strict attention is paid to the art of physical culture and to those outdoor sports which tend to develop the human body.

One of the leading organizations for physical culture and social intercourse in the Belleville Turnverein, and much of the popularity and growth of this organization is due to the able instructor, Prof. Christian L. Ebsen, who has held his position with the Turnverein since 1899.

Prof. Ebsen was born on the 26th of February, 1872, at Niebuell, Schleswig-Holstein, Germany, and is the son of Peter C. and Katherina Ebsen (nee Haldt). He attended the public school in Germany and also received private lessons. In 1888, when he was 16 years of age, he came to America and sought employment in Chicago. He found a position as lithographer and followed that line until 1897. During these years he was an active member of the Garfield Turnverein of Chicago and took advantage of all the opportunities for physical develop-

ment which that institution affo He during those days decided t come an instructor of physical cu and accordingly fitted himself for profession at the Normal Scho North American Gymnastic Unio Milwaukee. He graduated from institution in 1899.

The Belleville Turnverein wa that time looking for an able ins tor, and on recommendation of Emil Papprich Prof. Ebsen, who

Prof. C. L. Ebsen.

at that time instructor in Cederb Wis., was induced to come to B ville, and was made instructor of local organization. At that time t were but six classes in physical t ing in the Turnverein. Today t

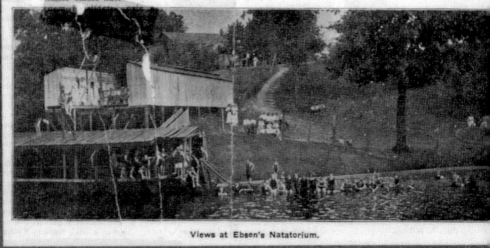

Views at Ebsen's Natatorium.

classes and all have a large ership.

g closely associated with every pertaining to sport and exer-tending toward physical devel-t, Mr. Ebsen saw the need of a rium for Belleville and accord-opened his resort on Lebanon in 1901.

eaters to the general public and d an able corps of attendants swimming instructions. Over swimmers have graduated from stitution since its inception. In to graduate it is necessary for dent to swim a distance of one e-half miles.

place is beautifully located and of the beauty spots of Belle-It is a family resort where the of Belleville can have all the

enjoyments of a bathing beach and summer resort without leaving Belleville.

Prof. Ebsen owns the natatorium and seven acres of ground surrounding it. He bought his property in 1902.

On the 15th of March, 1901, he was united in marriage with Miss Frances Wendt in Belleville. They are the parents of five robust and healthy children, named as follows: Ludolf C., Helga, Vilma, Norma and Herta.

He belongs to the following social and fraternal organizations: Royal Arcanum, Turnverein and Liederkranz.

Prof. Ebsen deserves the appreciation and gratitude of the people of Belleville for what he has accomplished in the way of physical culture.

Boys' Class, Belleville Turnverein.

The Baers Class, Belleville Turners.

spread, groups came from miles away, many from St. Louis. After a refreshing frolic in the waters of the pond, kegs of foaming cold beer were tapped in the grove of oaks and sycamores. Spreads of knackwurst and German potato salad were laid out, and as the beer flowed there was singing and dancing in the pavilion to a piano and boom bass. Romances blossomed and couples wandered the grounds. Occasionally, fights started but were quickly settled, because overall there still prevailed that overriding spirit of peacefulness and mellow happiness—German *gemütlichkeit*.

By 10:00 P.M., the last spooning couple was rounded up and all were loaded into their Overlands or Model Ts, Pierce Arrows, Kissel Kars or Surreys, and sent rolling home.

Then my father would lock up, douse the lights, and start the long trudge across the ravine to our new brick

(ABOVE) EBSEN SWIMMING SCHOOL, BELLEVILLE, ILLINOIS. THE SMALL STRUCTURE, TOP RIGHT, IS THE HOUSE IN WHICH I WAS BORN. 1910

(OPPOSITE) ME SHOWING OFF ALL MY SWIMMING MEDALS. 1926

house at 805 Lebanon Avenue, carrying a cigar box full of money, the day's "take" from pool admissions, bathing suit rentals, soda pop, ice cream cones and swimming lessons. I trotted along by his side as we abandoned the park to the custody of the stars, the crickets, the distant heat lightning, and the fireflies scrambling in the night.

I would strain my eyes examining each shadow ahead, the darkness behind each tree. On a leather thong on my wrist dangled my weapon, a "billy club" I had fashioned from a stout piece of oak. I was six but I was ready for immediate action, and I had cast myself in one of my first roles: I was my father's security guard.

When the war came, because Belleville was a predominantly German town and we were still neutral, there was some sympathy for the German cause. Once, after reading printed stories of German atrocities, including the bayoneting of Belgian babies, my father furiously twisted the paper into a crumpled wad and hurled it into the coal scuttle.

But in 1917, when it became our war and Scott Field was established near the sleepy little hamlet of Shiloh, four miles distant, frankfurters became hot dogs, and sauerkraut became liberty cabbage. Belleville opened its hospitable heart to the budding flyers and their French instructors in the operation of this newfangled flying machine, the JNC-4 or the "Jenny." When the first machines flew over, people ran out of their houses yelling "air-o-plane!" Normal business stood still while we craned our necks or lay on the grass and watched the thing maneuver until it was out of sight.

My father soon organized what today would have been a USO. He arranged dances at our park pavilion, and he gave ballroom dance instruction to the young soldiers in their recreation hall at the field. This attention to military needs produced the setting in which my *Tante* Marie found herself a husband.

Her choice was Carl Metcalf, a stalwart young mechanic in the 86th Aero Squadron. Carl was from Susanville, California, and, as kids do, we swarmed all over him. He had glamour. He was a soldier—a soldier in the Air Force. He told wondrous tales of hunting bears in the mountains of California. He had guns back there which he

MY *TANTE* MARIE AND "HER GUY," UNCLE CARL METCALF. 1918

promised to let me shoot one day. He was going to France to fight the Kaiser. He taught me how to roll Bull Durham cigarettes. Later, he taught me how to hunt squirrels, shoot a rifle and drive a car. He was a natural cutup, a little boisterous at times with a rollicking frontier spirit of the West, but to us kids, he was pure fun. My mother obliquely referred to him as "one of nature's noblemen." How our *Tante* Marie won him would always be something of a mystery to us because our aunt—a schoolteacher with a heart of gold and great spirit—was not a beauty. Although she was my mother's younger sister, she was actually verging on spinsterhood, and until the war came along and she helped my father teach the soldiers to dance, there was not a man in sight.

I think a certain chocolate cake had something to do with the capture, because I remember my mother and my aunt in the kitchen once conspiring and giggling like schoolgirls as they iced this cake. (I got to lick the spoon.) That night, they borrowed a horse and buggy and drove the four miles to Scott Field and passed the cake over the fence to my future Uncle Carl who was shipping out the next morning.

The winters in Belleville brought sledding and skating and roaring fires burning at the edge of the pond for thawing out. There was always plenty of ice and snow. Towards spring, February and March brought slush and pneumonia.

My mother was sick a lot. One day Dr. Barnburg had a long, serious talk with my father. After that, family rumors began to trickle down about a possible move to some warmer climate. California? Florida, maybe?

The thought of moving away brought me the ambivalent, poignant emotional wrenches probably felt most keenly by the young. I tend to be sentimental toward people and *anything* of long association. I don't like to throw things away. I loved the house we lived in, and every foot of the nine acres I had roamed ever since I could walk held a memory. I hated the thought of leaving my best friend Gustave Heineman, son of the grocer across the street. I would even miss the Stahlies. They were the multitudinous brood of a coal miner who lived nearby, and they constantly invaded our place like a Vandal horde of old. They were regularly repelled by me and my meager troops with a shower of crab apples, and once by my sister Helga wielding a buggy whip. The Stahlies didn't have a crab apple tree, so they threw rocks back.

Once, during a period of truce, they lured me into going swimming with them in the off-limits Richland Creek down by the L & N Railroad trestle. When they heard my *Tante* Marie (who was also their third grade teacher) calling and searching, they hastily got me dressed and dried my hair with their shirts, but we didn't fool her. When I got home my mother was waiting with my bag packed and an ultimatum: If I wanted to go swimming in filthy Richland Creek with the Stahlies instead of in the immaculate Ebsen pond, I could go and *live* with the Stahlies.

There was no contest. In the first place, the Stahlies barely had room for their own, so after some tears and a thorough scrubbing with laundry soap, I was allowed to stay. But I would always remember the free feeling of delicious wickedness swimming naked in Richland Creek with those "bad kids." And I can still feel the sandy bottom of that old creek under my feet.

Other memories flood my mind. I was up early one morning armed with bow and arrow, making my customary dawn patrol in search of bullfrogs, when I found a dead lady floating in the water.

The shock was heart-stopping. Evidently she had picked our pond to commit suicide. She was half sub-merged, her hands sticking out of the water—her eyes open. Neighbors said they had heard voices down there about midnight. Some said they had heard her praying.

It was traumatic. I ran all the way home. I hadn't seen many dead people, only poor little Herbie Muscoupf who had been accidentally shot through the heart with a .22 rifle by Pete Carbon while they were horsing around. And then there was that frozen tramp with his ragged grey beard point-ing to the sky that some people found down by the L & N water tank. I still remember the shrieking stillness of them. Then, as now, my spirit *rejects* death.

As an infant, I had spent a lot of time around railroad tracks. They tell me that at age two, after they had dragged the pond for me, I was found six blocks away at the L & N Railroad Station closely inspecting the wheels of a steam locomotive idling on a siding. And now, finally, with our family's move, I was to take a ride on a train.

It was going to be a long ride, all the way to Florida. I strolled up and down on the cinder sidewalk, where we had played marbles and "tippy," and in front of the vacant lot, where we coasted in the winter in front of our house at 805 Lebanon Avenue. I was in my new, short, military-type officer's coat holding court and accepting the goodbyes of friends and former foes: Gustav Heineman, the Stahlies, Pete Carbon, Raymond Carbon, even the neighborhood bully, Aloise Julious. Not much talk. Mostly mute looks and a feeling of poignancy and foreverness. A playmate was moving away.

A little girl asked me if I had kissed the house where I was born. It was a curious local children's rite I have never heard of since. But it was too late for that. The house I was born in had been torn down years ago and replaced with a tennis court.

Florida had won out over California as a place for us to move because Dr. Barnburg, a local physician, had a place in North Palm Beach, and a Belleville lady, Mrs. Mercker, had a house with a vacant apartment in West Palm Beach. Also, it was closer and less costly to get there.

Of the seven Ebsens, a beachhead was to be established by five: Mother, Norma, Vilma, Leslie, and me. Helga and Dad were to stay behind to wind up the business of selling the place, and since Dad was now the head of physical education for the Belleville Township High Schools, he would not be free to leave until June. Helga was at college in Indianapolis, and she had made a commitment to complete her school year.

After a gala supper and farewell gathering with our friends the Benignuses, and with the excitement of a great adventure, we piled into an Illinois Central sleeping car. I had never been farther away than St. Louis. We kids didn't sleep much that night, looking out at snowy fields and frozen rivers as the train puffed, rattled and rolled south. When we awakened we were in the red clay hills of Georgia, and the houses were on stilts. By late afternoon, the clay had given way to white sand and palm trees as we glided south down the Florida East Coast toward Palm Beach.

Back in 1893 an entrepreneur named Henry Flagler, upon his first visit to the as yet-undeveloped island of Palm Beach, had made a memorable utterance: "I have found a veritable Paradise." Twenty-seven years later an eleven-year old, fresh from the harsh frozen north, heartily endorsed Flager's finding. For me the place was unforgettable from the moment we stepped off one of Mr. Flagler's Florida East Coast railway cars into the balmy, skin-caressing night air.

Low-slung carbide gas lamps glided through the jasmine-scented darkness, as shiny-skinned black men propelled their wicker-chair tricycles down palm-lined pathways. A rising moon sprinkled silvery iridescence across the ripples of Lake Worth, and a low murmur of laughing voices rose and faded as attractive couples (undoubtedly millionaires), clothed in the soft cottons of summer, were pedaled along as occupants of the wicker-chaired vehicles.

The suddenness of this change of scene from Belleville impacted on me with the "sugar rush" of romantic enchantment, felt far beyond my years.

Later, when my bicycle arrived along with our crated furniture, I had the wheels to extend my cruising radius to every beckoning precinct of this new wonder-world.

First there was the water, with boats and the ocean for swimming: My first view of it was scary but addictive.

Then there was the fishing from the Breakers Pier for blue runners or from the edge of the gulf stream for grouper in a flat-bottomed skiff with my newfound friend, a powerful Bahamian black man named Sam.

There was the city dock where you could run errands for yachtsmen for a quarter tip, or even better, for a ride on one of their boats.

And there was Lake Worth for salvaging an abandoned rowboat. This single event was a milestone—or more appropriately a sea change, from when I was younger, standing on my homemade paddleboard holding a towel and feeling the breeze waft me across Dad's swimming pond. With the help of my new friend Doug Potter, whose family had a house with a pier on the West Palm Beach shore of Lake Worth, we dragged our waterlogged find up on his dock, and with some bamboo poles, some improvised leeboards, and one old bedsheet contributed by my mother, we converted this beauty into a sailing craft.

Christened *Sea Rover* and proudly launched, I immediately learned two cardinal imperatives toward achieving sailing satisfaction. First, your vessel must float. *Sea Rover* leaked, but not beyond the capacity of one full-time bailer.

CLEMATIS STREET, WEST PALM BEACH
WHERE I EARNED MY FIRST DOLLAR IN A SODA FOUNTAIN. 1920

Secondly, another sailboat gliding by you with apparent ease can spoil your day. One despised competitor did that, repeatedly, accompanying his maneuver each time with a sneering, superior smile. It was then I vowed that one day I would own the fastest sailing device afloat. I did—with my hot-rod catamaran *Polynesian Concept*—forty-eight years later.

We settled temporarily in a small apartment in West Palm Beach, but when my father arrived he quickly found a vacant house on what was then First Avenue (now Hammond Street) in Palm Beach, two blocks from Worth Avenue and fifty yards from the ocean. He bought it for $3,500. It was built on a raised footing, and beneath it I trapped skunks, much to the discomfort of my family.

I crammed a lot of living into that one year we lived there, and it was with jolting sadness that I received the

BREAKERS PIER, PALM BEACH, FLORIDA, 1910

news we were moving again.

But the economic realities were that Palm Beach was seasonal. My multifaceted and flexible father was now a dancing teacher, and while there was work in the winter, in the off-season the staples of our diet were coconuts and fish, much of which I supplied.

In 1921, Orlando, Florida, had a year-round base population of seven thousand, doubling or tripling during the winter tourist season. It was a beautiful little family town of lakes and big oak trees. When my father found it, he fell in love with the place, and betting it would grow and provide an ample field for his talents, we moved.

While in Orlando the now-vacant Palm Beach house burned down.

Dad went back to dispose of the lot and returned ecstatic: He had sold it for exactly what he had paid for the house and the land—$3,500. My father always had a good nose for real estate, but he also had bad timing: Today the lot is still vacant, but the eccentric old lady who owns it recently turned down $4 million for it.

Orlando was our home for the next seven years—critically decisive ones for me. It was during this time that I had to abandon my ambition to be a doctor (my cherished goal) for deep personal reasons.

My youngest sister Leslie had been stricken with epilepsy. Watching her seizures and suffering, and the travail it brought upon my parents, fueled my dedication toward medicine. Since there seemed to be no cure for Leslie's affliction, I idealistically decided I would become a doctor and find one.

Upon graduation from Orlando High School, I

enrolled in a pre-med course at the University of Florida. That was in the autumn of 1926.

Destiny, however, was working against my plan from the start.

The Great Depression, which peaked nationally—or rather bottomed—in 1929, had its beginnings in the collapse of the Florida land boom in 1926.

Forced by reduced economic circumstances to shift the scene of my studies from Gainesville to a school closer to home, my second year of higher education was spent as a day-student at Rollins College, just four miles from our front door.

Since Rollins, a liberal arts college, was shy of science

ROLLINS COLLEGE, WINTER PARK, FLORIDA. CIR. 1900

courses, my mother, playing a mysterious hunch, influenced me to complete my curriculum with an elective subject: drama.

Looking back on events, I ponder the coincidence that a Baptist Minister, Doctor Adcock, who had seen me in the High School Senior Class play, had asked me one day what I planned to do now that I had graduated. When I told him I was going to be a doctor, he said, "Too bad. The world has lost a great actor."

I can only assume other people saw potential in me that I did not fully recognize. Such a person was my journalism professor at Rollins, Willard Wattles. Here's what happened:

Hamilton Holt, the new president of the college, had a pet educational theory which he installed in the class-

rooms. Instead of arranging the student desks or armchairs in neatly squared rows, military fashion, with the professor up in front lecturing, the chairs or desks were arranged in a circle, with the professor or lecturer and students seated informally "in conference" as one group.

Doctor Holt heralded it as the "two-hour conference system." For my major thesis in the course I wrote about it rather irreverently under the title "Bull Session Education." It earned top marks in my journalism class.

President Holt, when presented with a copy, was not ecstatic, but Professor Wattles was. He asked me what I was going to do out in the world, and when I told him he said, "Well, whatever else you do—you are a *writer*."

I was an average student during my days at Orlando High School. Thanks to the head start I had in Belleville in my father's natatorium, I made the swimming team four years. I also made the football team my senior year, flunked Latin two years, and played saxophone in the school band.

I also broke into print in the *Daily Bulletin* with a short piece entitled "Spring Fever," considered by some of my chums to be my perpetual natural state.

In the spring of my year at Rollins I fell deeply in love.

She was twenty-seven. I was twenty. Her name was Beatrice. She had just been through the Reno divorce mill. Along with her five-year-old son, she had joined her parents for a visit.

Her father was president of the college I was attending, and we met at a fraternity tea dance. When I caught a glimpse of this golden-haired vision dancing in the arms of another, I had to cut in.

She looked up at me with an amused, questioning

smile that seemed to want an answer. So out of this twenty-year-old romantic came the words, "I was irresistibly drawn." The line must have been a cut above the average normal student dialogue because I could see it impacted.

We had a lot of dates.

Bystanders, not under the spell of moonbeams, orange blossoms and beauty, had no trouble predicting this matchup wasn't going anywhere, but it's a well-known fact that love is blind. So when she left suddenly for New York to marry again, I was devastated.

Psychologists declare that man's most compelling motivations are the quest for food and shelter, and some argue that ahead of those comes the quest for recognition. I can attest to the potency of a fourth: the drive "to show someone" who has rejected you.

The experience with Beatrice supplied the booster-rocket fuel for my already-planned success in New York. I would make her wish she had chosen *me*.

Four years later, to the stage door of the Imperial Theatre where I was enjoying my first real Broadway recognition, there came a letter. The handwriting was excitingly familiar.

It was from *her!* And the contents were warm and inviting.

But by then a funny thing had happened: I didn't care anymore.

MY ARRIVAL IN NEW YORK

If you had looked through the pages of the *New York Times* on August 4, 1928, you would have seen that Charles Lindbergh was still America's hero; Babe Ruth was hammering out home runs for the Yankees; Jack Dempsey, despite his loss to Tunney, was still the champion for the masses; Paul Whiteman was the King of Jazz; Ziegfeld was glorifying American girls; and Al Capone was taking over Chicago.

But there occurred another event on that date, unreported in the newspapers. The population of New York was increased by one because of the arrival from the south of a young man, twenty years old, six-foot-three, one hundred sixty-eight pounds—a youth full of wonder, fright and determination. His material assets were one cowhide suit-

TIMES SQUARE. 1920

case containing a change of underwear and socks, a couple of shirts, a toothbrush, a pair of tap shoes, and one yellow collegiate slicker with "Hot Dawg" penned on a sleeve. In the pants pocket of his dark suit was all his ready cash—$1.65. Inside his right sock below the shoe level, where he could feel its reassuring pressure, was his total cash reserve: two bills—a twenty and a five.

Carefully tucked away in the inside breast pocket of his jacket, he guarded one intangible asset, a letter of introduction to a friend of his ex-college roommate's cousin, who was a chorus boy in a show that was closing.

I was that young man and the $26.65 I carried was all that remained of the $50 I had borrowed for the trip from my solvent sister Norma (who then worked in a bank).

The probable Vegas morning betting line against my "making it" in New York City would have been, I figure, about a million to one; yet it never occurred to me that I might fail.

Confidence was the mystical ingredient among my assets. Without it there could have been no success.

When the day coach finally glided to a jerking halt and the conductor announced, "Pennsylvania Station, New York City," I picked up my belongings and stumbled off the train. Swirled along and up the platform by the buffeting human current, I gawked at the scene about me. In the many-tracked train shed where I found myself, the echoing noises of released air brakes, along with trains being called and trains moving about, reverberated in my ears. The smell was metallic and grimy. And underneath it all was another sound—the low, sustained roar of the city, the merging sounds of many vehicles and many people in motion.

As I walked, I felt my excitement grow, heightened by the ectoplasmic heat of so much humanity: many souls compressed into a gigantic surrounding city. My game plan called for stashing my impedimenta, finding the stage door of the Mansfield Theatre, and then locating the person to whom my letter of introduction was addressed.

The Pennsylvania Station checkroom was presided over by a large, scowling Red Cap, who gave me my first lesson in the fabled New York "sharp" practice. The sign over the checkroom plainly read, "Checkroom: 10¢ Per Article." Trying to save a precious dime, I stopped, unbuckled the heavy straps around my cowhide suitcase, and strapped my yellow slicker onto it. Then I placed the suitcase on the counter and put a dime beside it. The Red Cap, without hesitation, yanked my slicker from the straps, looked me coldly in the eye and said, "That'll be twenty cents." I reluctantly dug out another dime. Here was my very first negotiation in New York, and I already had been "out-slickered."

The Pennsylvania Station fronted on Eighth Avenue between Thirty-Second and Thirty-Third Streets. As I approached the street, although I had heard no sirens, it was quite apparent there had been an accident. Everybody was running. I craned my neck and tried to locate the scene. Then the lights changed, and I had to jump aside because everybody started running the other way. "My God," I thought, "there've been two accidents." Then it seeped in: This is the way people move in New York. So I took a deep breath, jumped in among them and started running, too. I didn't realize until I had gone several blocks that I was running the wrong way. The street numbers were getting smaller. Crossing town, I wound up on Park Avenue, and somewhere along the way I saw a building marked YMCA. I remembered my mother's words: "Son, spend your first night in New York in a YMCA." I went in but found I didn't qualify on three counts. First, it was a railroad man's YMCA. Second, I was neither a railroad man nor a YMCA member. And third, the room rates would have wiped out my cash reserve in forty-eight hours.

Continuing on Park Avenue to East Forty-Seventh Street, I turned left. I had a hunch Times Square was on the west side, and ten minutes later I emerged in that clearing of buildings where Broadway slices diagonally across Seventh Avenue, marking the famous center of the theater world, Times Square. I stood there in a daze reading the signs I had seen in ads in the theatrical section of the *New York Times*, while goofing off in the study hall back at school. Joe Cook in *Five and Dandy*, Fred and Adele Astaire in *Funny Face*, Eddie Dowling in *Honeymoon Lane*—and here I was, in the same world and on the same street where they were.

I found the stage door of the Mansfield Theatre. The doorman was traditional. He was a typical stage door "Pop" type. Small, balding, wearing bifocals, and smoking an underslung pipe. The company was rehearsing, he said. I asked to see Hank Ladd. He looked at me a beat, then disappeared. Two minutes later, he returned with a tall, pale, perspiring young man.

"Hank Ladd?" I asked. He nodded and I continued, "I'm Buddy Ebsen. I'm a friend of Lois Mark in Jacksonville. She asked me to give you this letter." Hank took the letter and read it, then looked at me. It was a look I will long remember. It was the most eloquent expression of mixed annoyance and compassion I have ever seen.

"Can you do a time step?" Hank asked.

"Yes," I said and started to do one.

"Come on," he cut me off. He turned, and I followed him up the two steps and into the theater.

The stage of the Mansfield Theatre was swarming with young men and women. The women were mostly in their late teens or early twenties. Some of the "young looking" men were twice my age. The auditorium was dark, but a border of lights in the flies provided light on stage. The boys, dressed mostly in slacks and T-shirts, and the girls, in various leg-revealing rehearsal clothes, were gathered in small groups trading dance steps. A tall, well-built young man seemed to be in charge. While the others wore metal taps and heel plates on their shoes, he wore wooden dancing clogs, the first I had ever seen. I was fascinated. He moved among the groups coaching, demonstrating. They all learned fast and deftly executed steps that were flashier and much more intricate than the homemade ones I had brought up from Orlando, Florida. My adrenaline began pumping. This was Broadway. I was in fast company.

"Whitey!" Hank got the attention of the young man with the clogs. Whitey came over. Hank jerked his head in my direction and said, "Go."

I did a time step, beginning with a single, then threw in some more complicated triples. Whitey watched my feet, raised his gaze to give me the briefest once-over and said, "Give him a gun" and turned away.

The production then playing at the Mansfield was a Marine Show, *Present Arms*. It had been produced by Lew Fields, half of the legendary Weber and Fields comedy team.

Having had a year's run in New York, the show was being recast for the road.

Even among chorus people there are varying strata of security and economic well-being. Some, with apartments in New York, chose not to go on the road. These gaps were being replaced with "road apples" such as, well, hopefully *me*. Those leaving the show gambled their chances of getting a new job with one of the dozen or so new musicals in preparation. They might even, like Hank Ladd, have the promise of a job from one of the new choreographers.

Elated at the prospect of landing a job on my first day in town, I wore blisters on my hands learning to do the manual of arms with a rifle while tap dancing. Hank Ladd was more than kind. He roomed with two other chorus boys at 352 West Eighty-Seventh Street. One of the roommates was leaving the following day, and I was invited to move in, but I still needed a place for that first night. Retrieving my suitcase and slicker from Penn Station, I carried them ten blocks to a small inexpensive hotel I had spotted on Forty-Second Street between Eighth and Ninth Avenue. Here, for $2, I got a room with a bed that came out of the wall.

Bright and early the next morning, I moved my stuff by subway to Hank's apartment then hotfooted it down to the Mansfield for rehearsals.

At Ye Eat Shoppe on Eighth, just around the corner from the theater, a person could get a simple meal for 50¢, and at the Automat on Times Square for even less. Ye Eat Shoppe had delicious blueberry pie for 10¢ with whipped cream on it for a nickel extra. Sometimes I splurged. For the next five days, this was my orbit: the Mansfield Theatre to rehearse, Ye Eat Shoppe or the Automat to eat, and 352 West

Eighty-Seventh to sleep. My cash reserve was diminishing, but that was of no consequence. I had a job.

Then came the crucial sixth day. I had been rehearsing without pay, according to the chorus equity management contract that allowed a producer to rehearse a chorus person six days without compensation. If I was called back for the seventh I would either have a job or two weeks' salary. I was confident. Everyone seemed to like me. I had mastered the routines. The stage manager, Teddy Hammerstein, was friendly in a gruff, New York way. I felt I was in.

The sixth day at ten o'clock in the morning, producer Lew Fields arrived. He was there to OK the new people. He took a seat out in front of the stage, and we started a run-through. We finished the opening, and Teddy Hammerstein was summoned out front. The conversation between Hammerstein and Fields, repeated to me afterwards, went something like this:

"Who's the *longa loksh* that's six inches taller than anybody else," Fields asked Hammerstein.

"Oh, he's a good type. Just up from Florida."

"Get rid of him," Fields said. "He don't match."

I remember Teddy Hammerstein, a little guy, putting his arm around my shoulders as high as he could reach and walking me from the stage door to the street, where he stuck out his hand. "Sorry kid," he said, and we shook hands. When I took my hand away there were two dollar bills in it. I lived on that for the next three days. Toward the end of the fourth day, I was down to a quarter.

There used to be a Pennsylvania Drug Store on the northeast corner of Seventh Avenue and Forty-Eighth Street that sold candy. I thought, I'll get two Hershey bars, a nickel apiece. Then I'll go to a place I know on Sixth Avenue and get a giant chocolate malted (which was really mostly air). The malt was a dime. This'll leave me with the nickel subway fare to get to Eighty-Seventh Street.

As I was paying for the Hershey bars, I felt a tap on my shoulder. I turned and saw Hugh McKnight; I had graduated with him from Orlando High School back in Florida.

"Hi, Buddy Ebsen!" Hugh said. "What're you doin' up here?"

"Lookin' for work."

"Want to jerk soda?" Hugh asked.

"Sure."

"Go down and see Saul Fox, head of personnel at Pennsylvania Drug." He gave me the address, and two days later I was jerking soda at that very fountain. Then they shifted me to the Long Island Concourse, a hole-in-the-wall fountain just off the Long Island train platform.

The commuters poured in each morning, four deep at the bar, wanting coffee and bran muffins all at the same time. In the evening, between 4:30 and 5:00 P.M., the human tide was in again, with people fortifying themselves against a possible breakdown on the notoriously unreliable Long Island Railway—all wanting their chocolate malteds at the same time. It was the world's fastest fountain, and I was the world's slowest soda jerker.

My salary was $25, more than I had ever earned before. Each week I saved ten. I could do this because the closet-sized room I had moved into on the fourth floor of the 352 address cost $6, and I ate a lot of bran muffins together with very thick chocolate malteds when I arrived at work and just before leaving.

I was employed at the Long Island Concourse fountain for five weeks. I worked the night shifts, four o'clock to midnight. The fountain manager's name was Murray. He was short, dark-haired, dark-eyed, and doubtful of me from the start. In his view, I was slow and dumb.

New York was on daylight-saving time. On the big clock in the waiting room were two sets of hands, one red to indicate daylight-saving time, the other black, for eastern standard time. I used to get confused and once sat in the waiting room reading the *Daily News* for an hour, which got me to work at five, exactly one hour late. In Murray's silent look at my explanation, I read his thoughts. "This *schlemiel* has got to go!"

In the three years before coming to New York, I had physically grown fast. The muscle growth in my feet had not kept up with the bone structure, causing the keystone bone of one foot and then the arch in the other foot to slip down. It was extremely painful and required taping corrective pads to my feet; finally, I had to wear steel arch supports inside specially made orthopedic shoes. Before I left Florida to hit New York and become a dancer, I was on crutches. Now I was standing on my feet eight hours a day "slinging slop." The pain was getting to me. I asked Murray for a day off. He said scornfully, "Sure. Take a day off. Take a week off. Take a year. Better yet, don't come back at all." I decided to stand the pain a little longer.

New York had seven daily newspapers then. I favored the *Daily News*. It chronicled the day's events succinctly and was handy to carry and read on the subway. More important, it fit neatly inside the front of my buttoned-up jacket as I leaned into the chilly winds from the Hudson, staving off pneumonia those three blocks from the Eighty-Sixth Street subway exit to 352 West Eighty-Seventh Street. It was October, and I wouldn't have saved enough for an overcoat for another month.

One day, my three-cent investment in the *Daily News* paid off in yet another way. "Wanted," the small blurb on the theater page read, "singers and dancers for new Ziegfeld Show. Apply New Amsterdam Theatre 10:00 A.M. Monday."

There it was. This tiny fateful wisp of information. And there was I at the New Amsterdam at 10:00 A.M. sharp the following Monday morning.

Whoopee, a musical version of Owen Davis's play, *The Nervous Wreck*, had a western locale. Unlike Lew Fields's show, where the chorus had to match, choreographer Seymore Felix and librettist director William Anthony McGuire wanted disparate cowboy types. In the eight dancers finally selected, they had chosen Gil White, Frank Erickson, Joe Minatello, "Obie" O'Brien, Harold Ettus, "Chizzy" Mehan, "Red" Hughes and me. We were as disparate as our names!

Since my hours at the soda fountain were from 4:00 P.M.

to midnight, and the calls at the theater occupied the mornings, during the first week of my dual involvement I never had to be in two places at the same time. Then came the contretemps: The fatal sixth day fell on a Monday. If I received that crucial callback for the seventh day and had to start rehearsing at night, what would I do about my job?

I knew. I would quit. But I had to decide the manner of it. There was a moral issue involved. Saul Fox and the Pennsylvania Drug Company had been square with me, and I wanted to be square with them. But two weeks' notice would blow my new job in show business. And so I learned another lesson of the world. If the pressures are right, people will always find a way to rationalize, to justify, to ease their conscience in order to condone their conduct. The key was Murray. "Take a year," he had said, "or better yet, don't come back at all." And that's what I did. I was doing him a favor. I called in and left him a message that delivered the news. I figured he would celebrate with the added satisfaction of knowing he wouldn't have to pay me for Monday.

THE OUT-OF-TOWN TRYOUT

The special train that carried *Whoopee* to Pittsburgh included ten carloads: three of scenery, one of animals and six filled with people. The company mood after six weeks of concentrated rehearsal was a feeling of holiday for most, sleepless, excited anticipation for some, and carnival for the uninhibited few. Amid the laughter, drinking and berth hopping, I moved in a happy daze, observing, recording and trying to realize that here I was, a twenty-year old, fresh out of Florida via a soda fountain in Penn Station, thrust into the very center of Florenz Ziegfeld's glamour factory. I was part of a company of the planet's most photographed women and publicized talent and was being carried to further peaks of excitement promised by the world premiere of a Broadway-bound musical comedy. Not just any stage comedy. A Ziegfeld musical comedy.

BUDDY AND VILMA EBSEN. 1933

As the train rolled westward, I reviewed events of the past three months, looking back, and down, from my secure new heights of experience-bred sophistication at the green kid who got off the train August 4th in the Big Town. Here it was only October, and I was already earning $45 a week! Some bank vice presidents in depression-plagued Florida would have been glad to make that. No more 3¢ tabloids under my jacket to ward off the cold. I could now afford the *Sunday Times*—*and* an overcoat. No more Automat, unless of course, I wanted a good cup of coffee and a moment's repose to study the people. Now I could dine whenever I desired, sometimes at Caruso's Spaghetti Palace just off Times Square, or at Ye Eat Shoppe and have blueberry pie with whipped cream for a nickel more. I could study my dancing role models, Bill Robinson and John Q. Bubbles, from a balcony seat at the Palace as often as they played there. God was good and I thanked Him.

All of this whirled through my head as we glided at reduced speed through Pennsylvania towns, and I listened to my seatmate, the show's second comic Will Philbrick, narrate a travelogue. Will was a veteran character actor who had taken me under his wing to impart a few elementary things about show business. "Played this burg in 1908," he reminisced, pointing out the window. It was awesome: 1908 was the year I was born. "Minstrel show, doubled in brass. See that street? Main Street. We paraded down that Main Street every night to lead people to the theater. Town hasn't changed much." I drank it all in and envied him for the richness of his experience.

The old Nixon Theatre, cater-cornered from the William Penn Hotel (a forty-story aluminum monument to commerce stands here today), was to be the site of the *Whoopee* opening. The Nixon was a fine theater with the built-in resonance of a rare old musical instrument. I know that within its ancient walls and its dark recesses there dwelt backstage ghosts of the Victorian past. I am sure when the theater was "dark" they came out, and by the eerie illumination of its single work light, they replayed their triumphs in *The Count of Monte Cristo, Hamlet,* or *Forty-five Minutes from Broadway,* taking bows to the echo-chambered applause of a ghostly audience. But for now the ghosts were displaced, giving way to the flesh and blood and bustle of a new show. Our show. *Whoopee.*

To assign dressing rooms, without totally disrupting the company, required the wisdom and judgment of a Solomon, plus the authority of a Supreme Court. This delicate chore fell to sensitive assistant stage manager Frank Colletti who consulted with his boss Zeke Colvin, a gray, dour rock of a man with a wry sense of humor. I discovered later that his altogether forbidding exterior covered a soft heart. One thing Zeke knew: No matter how carefully and judiciously he assigned dressing rooms, he could bet the rent money on one sure thing—nobody was going to be happy.

We, who were dignified in the program as "gentlemen of the ensemble" (actually, chorus boys), were assigned a large communal dressing room beyond the musicians' room and the wardrobe department, in the nethermost reaches of the basement. At stage level nearest to the stage was a posh dressing room with a private bath and a star on the door occupied by Eddie Cantor, our show's star. Ranging onward and upward according to salary, billing, or contractual stipulation were the dressing rooms of the other principals. On the second floor was a large room similar to ours that served the twenty-four dancing girls, and above on the third floor was the dressing room for the twelve "long-stemmed American beauty" showgirls.

Over their protests, the showgirls were placed far from the stage on the logical premise that they had fewer entrances and exits; their most telling appearance came in the finale of Act One when they rode Indian ponies down a ramp around a mountain, bare-bottomed except for G-strings, and with full-feathered Indian war bonnets on their heads.

Most of the principals and higher salaried members of the company took advantage of a theatrical rate and stayed at the William Penn. Dancer Frank Ericson knew of a boarding house in the low-rent district of Pittsburgh where we could get a room for $6 a week. We roomed there together. Where we slept was unimportant because with endless rehearsals scheduled, we would be just about living at the theater. Who would want to be anywhere else while a Broadway show was being assembled?

A call to the theater did not mean we were constantly on our feet dancing. There were long intervals during which the massive Joseph Urban scenery was being jockeyed about, backdrops were being hung, and lights were being clamped to the balcony rails amid endless shouting back and forth by strangers. Principals were rehearsing scenes in the lobby of the theater. Our director, William Anthony McGuire, laughed at the clever way Eddie Cantor rolled his eyes, making a funny line even funnier. Ethel Shutta, an Oklahoma-born straight-woman trained in burlesque, was a tower of strength on stage: deft, poised, sure, and a perfect foil for Cantor, her reactions making him funnier. She was a lady who delivered, knew her worth, and was not to be pushed around by anybody. There was much to be learned by simply watching. Volumes! I was privileged, and I knew it, and I thought shyly of the day when I, too, might be a principal.

About a year later, William Anthony McGuire stopped me on the way out of the Amsterdam Theatre and said, "You've got a great personality, kid. Someday I'm going to have a part for you." I had no way of knowing then, that years downstream, he would keep his promise at MGM Studios in the film *Girl of the Golden West.*

As the deadline of an 8:30 P.M. opening-night curtain approaches, tempers get short. The costumes don't fit, the overcrowded dressing rooms stink, and there's no time to make changes. The scenery is too big, a prop is missing, the orchestrations are in the wrong key, and all the while, the clock keeps ticking.

About 2:00 A.M., at the peak of chaos, Ziegfeld went into action. Agitation cranking his pipes into a high-pitched whine, Ziegfeld peeled off his coat, loosened his tie, and took charge. "Uh-oh," Harold Ettus whispered to me, "Ziggy's going to do his act."

"A hundred goddamn directors around here and nobody knows their ass from a hole in the ground," Ziegfeld growled. "Morris!" he shouted to the lighting booth above, "Gimme a magenta!"

Out of the frozen silence came a noise from Cantor like a choking sob. "Flo," he said in an imploring, yet accusing tone. "You can't play comedy in the dark!"

"In my shows, Cantor, the audiences don't come for comedy. They come to see my girls," Ziegfeld answered as he proceeded to relight the show. Cantor stomped off to his dressing room in despair.

The most neglected part of every musical show in my experience has been the finale, on the theory that if you haven't captured the audience by then, it's too late anyway. In *Whoopee*, this neglect was carried to the ridiculous. At 4:00 A.M. before opening night the finale had not only been unrehearsed, its music had not even been written. Panic!

In Ziegfeld's present mood, the situation was perilous. Heads could roll. The company united. While someone momentarily distracted Ziggy, Paul Florenz, the assistant stage

FROM LEFT TO RIGHT: OSCAR HAMMERSTEIN II, PRODUCER FLORENZ ZIEGFELD, AND JEROME KERN DURING THE ORIGINAL PRODUCTION OF "SHOWBOAT." 1927

manager, hastily gathered the entire chorus around the piano where lyricist Gus Kahn frantically scribbled words on a sheet of paper. He wrote some lyrics as fast as his fingers could push the pencil and laid the sheet before Walter Donalson, seated at the piano. Donalson, the complete pro, momentarily put aside his propensity to romance every cutie in the chorus line and coolly improvised a thirty-two bar chorus that perfectly fit the lyrics. Forgettable, perhaps, but adequate. The singers learned it on sight, and we dancers reprised a routine to it that we had done earlier in the show. Through our teamwork we had glossed over and covered up a nasty situation; apparently Ziegfeld was never the wiser.

George Olsen provided the music for *Whoopee.* His band played in the pit until just before the finale when they crept one by one through the musicians' crawl hole into a backstage area, then reappeared on a bandstand on stage where they played for the rest of the show. George was Ethel Shutta's husband. During a lull in the staging of the finale, Ethel had drifted over to George, and the two were engaged in quiet conversation when Ziegfeld's voice came from out front.

"Hey, you!"

Its harshness and high decibel level commanded silence. "Yeah, you!" he restated, when Ethel looked up. He pointed a finger at her so there could be no mistake. Ethel was cool and quiet, but we all heard the words.

"Were you addressing me—sir?"

"I don't want talking on stage while I'm directing out here," Ziegfeld commanded.

Ethel glanced at her husband, then strolled down to the footlights, stopped, and stared out at Ziegfeld. When she spoke, she did not raise her voice. Her delivery was measured, clear, firm and forceful.

"Listen, you gray-haired old son of a bitch," she said. "I'll talk to my husband any goddamn time, any goddamn place I want to. You're not Jesus Christ to me." Then emphasizing with a jabbing forefinger, she said, "And *don't you forget it.*"

She waited a beat for a rebuttal. When none came, she strolled calmly back to her husband and resumed the conversation. For a full minute, no sound broke the stunned silence in the auditorium. Finally, there was a vague stirring of movement and low conversation out front. I was stricken, in shock. There were tears in my eyes. In my mind's eye, I was seeing the death of this project. All this money spent, energy wasted, and dreams shattered. Mine in particular. Now there wasn't going to be any show. After the scene I had just witnessed, how could there be? My despair was interrupted by dance director Seymore Felix's voice.

"All right, let's take it from where the girls enter." And the rehearsal went on. The show went on. The out-of-town notices were good. The New York opening was a smash, and *Whoopee* ran for a year and a half.

Ruby Keeler

The company was on a dinner break. With two other enthusiasts, I returned to the rehearsal hall early to beat the lumps out of one of the more difficult steps—when she entered.

Continuing with our individual hoofing problems, we remained aware of her, watching from the corners of our eyes as she staked her spot on one of the benches, shed her slacks, and revealed those traffic-halting legs. She then

removed neat wooden-soled dancing shoes from her carrying case, tied them on, and stood, displaying a slim, perfectly proportioned body. Her fresh young Irish face was lit with large, blue eyes, which sparkled with self-assurance. When she started to dance, we stopped.

After a few brief warm-up steps, she began an intricate Jack Blue tap routine, handling it with complete mastery. If there is such a thing as love at first sight, that's what was happening to me.

Harold Ettus, our source for all general and private information, sidled over to me. Almost in answer to what must have been a slack-jawed look on my face, he said, "Yeah, that's Ruby Keeler. She's seventeen. Right out of Texas Guinan's nightclub. She's gonna play the ingenue. All the guys in town are nuts about her. Johnny Irish, one of the 'boys,' has the inside track. Al Jolson wants to marry her, but he's asking for cement overshoes, if you ask me. If Al wins, she won't be in the show long."

Harold's call was correct. Jolson won Ruby after she captivated audiences for only three weeks, just as she had captured me in those first three minutes. She left the show for Hollywood as Mrs. Al Jolson, leaving us potential suitors to cope with our flaming torches.

In Hollywood, Ruby's talents quickly took her to starry heights, and later Broadway validated her stardom in *Show Girl* and *No, No, Nanette*. Eventually, due to overwork some said, came that ugly robber—Ruby suffered a stroke.

Time cut: Forty-eight years later.

I was shooting a picture in the Monterey, California, area with my costar John Ritter when my secretary called. The Masquers Club in Hollywood was honoring Ruby with a testimonial dinner, and they wanted me to be the presenter of the plaque. This was a surprise because our paths had not crossed since the *Whoopee* days.

I sent my sincere regrets, since the shooting schedule prohibited my presence. I had put the matter behind me. But later that evening, after a superb dinner in Cannery Row, my insistent inner urging could not be denied. I wrote this poem inspired by the memory of my first sight of Ruby—that day she had walked into our rehearsal hall:

> *To the sparkle of a diamond*
> *Add the soft warm glow of pearl.*
> *Then add a smile from the Emerald Isle,*
> *And shape it like a girl.*
> *Then find a perfect sapphire*
> *And confiscate the star.*
> *Now add the best of all the rest*
> *Of precious gems there are.*
> *Then if you live in Oz*
> *And have the power of the Wiz,*
> *You may wind up with half*
> *The precious jewel that Ruby is.*

I mailed it to my daughter Bonnie, having made arrangements for her to represent me at the dinner. Her rendition of the poem created what is known in Hollywood as "a moment."

Ruby cried. She kept the original copy.

Eddie Cantor

In his book *My Life Is in Your Hands*, copies of which Eddie Cantor inscribed and presented to every member of the *Whoopee* company for Christmas in 1928, he speaks of his beginnings as a performer. As a skinny urchin with big eyes, he roamed the streets of New York's lower East Side and discovered that by making funny faces and rolling his large eyes he could elicit smiles and laughter, and sometimes even coins, from passersby. With his native talent for comedy, personally discovered by Gus Edwards, he eventually found himself in a vaudeville act with two other kids also destined to become world famous: Walter Winchell and Georgie Jessel.

Later he worked as a singing waiter in beer gardens at Coney Island with a young Jimmy Durante at the piano. They would entertain the customers, often by ad-libbing requested songs when the original didn't come to mind. It was probably then that Cantor picked up his sprightly ambulating style, ever-moving, and bouncing constantly from one side of the stage to the other from the discovery, no doubt, that a moving target is harder to hit!

Having come up the hard and honest way, Eddie had a deep understanding of and regard for human beings. I found him to be a caring, compassionate and vulnerable man. When the *Whoopee* baseball team, which was recruited from the cast, first played ball in Central Park against other stage shows, it was in need of uniforms and equipment. Cantor bought them. When we were in Chicago, a skinflint theater manager shut off the work-lights, so we chorus kids could no longer practice on stage during the day. Eddie

changed that. "For any kid ambitious enough to work his or her way out of the chorus," he said, "I will pay for the lights." My sister and I were especially grateful.

Eddie also gave me my first lines to speak on a Broadway stage at the Amsterdam Theatre. It was late during the run of *Whoopee*, and Ethel Shutta left the show, taking along her brother Jack. That left a small part to be played in one of the scenes, and Eddie promoted me from the chorus to play that part. I'll always remember that.

EDDIE CANTOR POSSIBLY REACTING
TO ZIEGFELD'S RE-LIGHTING OF THE SHOW.

Incidentally, I saw him in tears twice. Once was when Ziegfeld personally re-lit *Whoopee* before the opening night in Pittsburgh. The second time was closing night in Cleveland when, after an eighteen-month run, he joined the weeping show girls as they hugged and kissed their farewells on the stage after the final curtain.

Due to the drifting, mystic currents of destiny, I did not see Eddie again for thirty-five years. He was dying of a heart ailment at his home in Beverly Hills, and I was starring in "The Beverly Hillbillies." My agent Jimmy McHugh, who had married one of Eddie's daughters, arranged for me to see him again after all those years. His lifelong friend Georgie Jessel was in the room and both seemed moved emotionally that I had come. Remembering his past kindnesses, Eddie's frailty and faint voice brought tears to my eyes. I recalled his vitality as he cavorted nightly about the Amsterdam stage, captivating sold-out audiences. I remembered the awe in which we chorus kids held him. He was a star! And he earned the fantastic sum of $5,000 a week. *Five thousand*! And then I realized the meaning of the American dream and was filled with gratitude and with wonder that I, a lowly chorus dancer in his show, could dream of achieving such heights in this fabulous country of ours.

ATLANTIC CITY

The morning after the national elections of 1976, in answer to the question "Who won in New Jersey?" somebody said, "The William Morris office."

What it meant was that since the citizens of New Jersey had voted to legalize gambling, Atlantic City stood to become Las Vegas East. And the Morris office, traditional peddler of the industry's top casino attractions, stood to reap a bumper golden harvest from its ten-percents of the fabulous salaries these top attractions command. My beginning salary there was $10.

I first saw Atlantic City in the summer of 1929 from the window of a coach in the shore train from Philadelphia. As we approached the salt marshes that separate the sand spit the city stands on from the mainland, the late-afternoon

BENNY DAVIS. 1931

sun picked up rosy glints from the low line of buildings that were the city's skyline. Here and there a more substantial boardwalk hotel interrupted the silhouette of the predominantly beach-shack architecture. To me it was a new and strange place—but it didn't scare me. It had the feeling of other beach towns I knew, like Daytona. And the salt marsh smell in my nostrils was reassuring, comforting, and probably due to the mysteries of heredity—like a homecoming.

I had good vibrations from this place, and they were prophetic. Atlantic City was to become a memorable landmark among the events of my life.

A good part of my secure feeling in this new place was because I would not be alone. My sister Vilma was here, and she had a job. How this came to be is complicated and includes some of the elements of a Cinderella story—in reverse.

I was in *Whoopee*, and since any Eddie Cantor hit was traditionally good for a year, maybe two, I felt economically secure enough to bring Vilma to New York, according to plan, to launch her career. The first thing I did after she arrived was to enroll her in the Jack Donahue-Johnny Boyle School of Dancing located on the fifth floor of the Gallo Theatre building.

It hadn't taken me long since my arrival to realize that, while a certain innocence in our homemade dance steps was refreshing and crowd pleasing, what we needed was a little "meat" to go with our "home fries." We needed steps—and Johnny Boyle had them. He was a walking and dancing catalogue of all the steps, traditional or newly invented, that any hoofer had ever danced since the year one, and he executed them to perfection. I had arrived in

New York too late to see Boyle and Donahue as a vaudeville team, but the legend was that Johnny could dance rings around Jack. Jack was the salesman, the personality that made the act click with the charm that led to Ziegfeld stardom, while Johnny loyally cheered him on from the wings.

Vilma, with her charm, talent and quickness was an immediate sensation at the Boyle-Donahue dancing school, so when Johnny was called upon to doctor the choreography of the Vincent Youmans musical, *Great Day*, which was trying out in Atlantic City, he took with him four of his most promising pupils. Vilma was one of them, and she departed ecstatically with the Boyle group for Atlantic City—and her first job in show business. Johnny's four promising pupils were to replace four girls in the show, but the shoes of the girl Vilma was to replace didn't fit. So the girl stayed in the show. And Vilma got her first lesson in the heartbreaking vagaries, disappointments, illogical road blocks, and fickle-fingered threads of fate, woven in recurrent, often idiotic design through the vast tapestry of show business.

After her shattering rejection by the economy-minded management of *Great Day*, Vilma sought comfort and some repose on that section of the beach frequented by chorus kids and entertainers from the Atlantic City nightclubs. There Vilma chanced to meet Frank McCormick, a happy-go-lucky young Irish hoofer who was working as MC at the Blackstone Hotel supper club. Frank introduced her to his bosses, Mr. and Mrs. Joe Moss, and the next night Vilma replaced a girl in that show whose shoes fit her perfectly. In addition to working in the line, the job called for the performance of one specialty solo. So Vilma came through with a *nautch* dance, performed with a prop (a one-string oriental guitar) exactly as she had done it in Dad's most recent dance recital in Orlando. The *nautch* dance is traditionally performed by Hindu dancing girls, its subtle movements designed to titillate. Instead of titillation, Vilma substituted a winning smile. The dance was so innocent, and Vilma was so charming that it riveted the sophisticated audiences, especially the drunks at the 4:00 A.M. show.

"Nucky" Johnson, the "boss" of Atlantic City, came in one night and, as was his custom, invited all the girls in the show to his large table for champagne. Being an exceedingly generous man and a gracious host, it was also his custom upon departing to leave each girl with a fistful of twenty dollar bills.

One morning Vilma approached me with a big smile, waving four "horse blanket" sized twenty dollar bills, green on one side and yellow on the other, meaning redeemable in gold (which was the case in those days).

I said, "Where'd you get those?" I knew it wasn't payday. She told me that Nucky Johnson had given them to her. I said, "Give them back."

Hurt, she said, "Why? We can use the money: Dad wants to come up to Atlantic City, and it would pay his fare."

I said, "Give the money back, or I'm putting you on the next train to Orlando, Florida." And that was that.

I never met Nucky Johnson, only had him pointed out to me from a distance. I like to imagine that this freewheeling, free-spending city boss of a resort town was haunted by a baffling memory of something that took place there during Prohibition—something akin to Citizen Kane and Rosebud: a memory of a pretty girl who approached him in front of a nightclub one night, thrusting four twenty dollar bills into his hand, barely blurting out, "My brother won't let me keep them," as she turned away and ran like hell.

The landmark character of Atlantic City, as it pertained to our destined careers, occurred in this way:

In September, when Atlantic City shut down, and *Whoopee* resumed, I brought Vilma back to New York and successfully maneuvered her into the show.

With our added experience and the acquisition of new steps, using the mellow maple apron of the Amsterdam stage as a daily practice space, we put together a three-chorus dance routine that was to become our show-stopping vehicle to success.

Whoopee closed in Cleveland the following February.

Transported back to New York, Vilma and I lost no time in seeking exposure for our new dance routine.

Through the good offices of Mr. and Mrs. Joe Moss, Vilma's bosses in Atlantic City, we secured an audition with a man named Benny Davis.

Benny had an act called *Broadway Stars of the Future*, which was populated by ambitious youngsters like ourselves who had measured up to Benny's standards, eliciting his somewhat mystic appraisal, i.e., "This kid's got something."

Our audition was a fiasco. It was held at ten o'clock

in the morning, without music, in the cold, empty Hollywood Restaurant in New York City.

The result? "I'll take the girl," said Benny.

Vilma always captivated.

To me he gave some pertinent advice. "Kid," he said, "Light up your pan." What he meant was that I had to smile more.

We did not see Benny again for six months.

Frustrated by his rejection of us as a team, we returned to Orlando to star in our father's annual dance recital and bask for a while in our roles as hometown celebrities, "Orlando's own Broadway stars."

We accepted the accolades, knowing that the billing was inflated. Meanwhile, we quietly determined to go back up there to Yankee Land and make the billing for real.

Vilma was not long out of action.

There came a wire from Jack Pomeroy, a nightclub show producer and chance acquaintance met during her Atlantic City summer. With his wife, choreographer Josephine Earl, he was producing a show for a small cafe, the Babette Club in Atlantic City; he wanted to know if Vilma would come up and work for them. She did, and this time our positions were exactly reversed. Vilma went up first and established the beachhead, then sent me the fare.

I arrived in Atlantic City on July 4, 1930, and moved into the apartment Vilma shared with the adagio trio, Theodore, Enrica and Novello, in addition to two of Vilma's showgirl friends. I slept on the couch, loafed on the beach, developed a healthy tan, and watched Vilma work.

I felt shamelessly useless.

A friendly vaudevillian I had met on the beach suggested I create a single comedy dance act for myself, trying burlesque, which was a great school for entertainers, boasting graduates like Bert Lahr and Fanny Brice.

I had already been experimenting along these lines toward a blackface character dressed in ill-fitting, decadent elegance who opens with the song "Just a Gigolo" and gets off with a comic eccentric dance routine.

It was a solid, basic concept, but one that would have taken months of rehearsal and playing time to perfect. In desperation I auditioned cold, *sans* audience, for the minstrel show playing on the Million Dollar Pier. Nothing worked.

It was a disaster. My spirits, already low, hit bottom. Then, one Saturday morning Vilma approached me with a twinkle in her eye.

"How're you feeling?" She asked.

"So-so." My hand gesture showed little enthusiasm.

"Well get yourself together," she said. "We're going on tonight."

What she had done was talk Blanche Babette, owner of the club, into letting Vilma, after her specialty performance in the show, introduce me and do an encore with "her little brother just up from Florida." For this appearance I was to get $10. Naturally I acquiesced. I was not particularly nervous or excited about performing. The phlegmatic Ebsens were always cool—never lit up until they heard their music.

Our number was choreographed to the popular standard "Ain't Misbehavin'," that great tune featured and made popular by Louis Armstrong. And the little five-piece club band knew it well. The jazzy trumpet player even played it as though Armstrong had personally schooled him.

Our sold-out audience was a typical Saturday night

beach crowd. Attractive, suntanned women in summery dresses. Husbands down for the weekend, happy escapees from their jobs in sweltering Philadelphia. All raring for an evening on the town.

Halfway into the show, which was going well, Vilma did her solo, a little Johnny Boyle buck dance. "And now," Vilma said after the applause, "would y'all like to meet my little brother just up from Florida?"

Of course they would. Our music started and out came "little brother," all six foot three of me, which drew a warm chuckle from the audience.

Using a device popular with the hoofers I had seen at the Palace, we began our routine with an eight-bar rhythmic walk-around, sort of establishing a "tapsichorean" parameter for the action to follow—and then we broke into the dance.

The first step was derived from the familiar Charleston dance moves, but amplified. Contrasting suddenly and sharply with the restrained "walk around," it packed shock value. By the sixth bar the audience broke into spontaneous applause. This gawky boy, all arms and legs, and this beautiful girl making a pattern of surprising moves in a perfect expression of the music was something they had never experienced before.

The ripple of applause signifying acceptance was all we needed.

The dam broke. My pan lit up. We danced our hearts out, and by the time we reached the third chorus and the eight-bar exit step with the band blasting the "ride out," the audience was applauding, whistling, and shouting their approval so loudly that we could hardly hear the music.

Vilma and I were letter-perfect in our routine, since we had practiced it for almost a year. It was indeed what news media circles describe as the "Big Story." "A room full of gas and someone strikes a match."

The explosion didn't stop until, having no encore, we had to repeat the last chorus of the dance—twice—and then beg off with heartfelt thank-yous.

Now came the big surprise—the topper. The first person in the congratulations line was a vaguely familiar face—Benny Davis—wearing a much different expression than when we saw him last. His face was a picture of affability. He attempted a totally unnecessary introduction to the man with him—Walter Winchell, Mr. Broadway—who was then the most powerful columnist in the history of the newspaper business, a man courted by beggars, tycoons and presidents for a kind word or just a crumb of recognition.

"You kids are great," Walter said. "Watch my column."

Benny looked stricken. "But wait, Walter," he pleaded, "I haven't got them signed yet." A burgeoning crowd of well-wishers descended upon us, and they were lost in the confusion.

Walter didn't wait. The next day in the *New York Daily Mirror* the Winchell "rave" was so filled with accolades that it brought us offers of employment from coast to coast. Suddenly we were up to our hips in opportunistic agents, not to mention a worried and frustrated Benny Davis who now haunted us nightly, waving a contract in hopes that we would sign.

We thought it through, weighed the alternatives, and came to a wise and surprisingly mature decision for people so young. It was flattering to be wanted, but despite our overnight success we realized that we needed the seasoning we would get by touring vaudeville houses with Benny Davis. So one night I gave him the news. "Benny," I said. "Light up your pan. We're going with you."

The time was August, 1930. I was twenty-two years old. Looking back over events long past, I continuously find support for my belief that the future is far more amazing than you can possibly imagine it.

During the period immediately after Vilma's and my "discovery" by Walter Winchell at the tawdry little Babette Club in Atlantic City, there was an interval during which Benny Davis and his cute and energetic wife Dorothy took us under their protective and possessive wings.

We were constant, often overnight, guests at their Park Avenue apartment. We were chauffeured in their

WALTER WINCHELL. 1932

twelve-cylinder Packard limousine by their congenial Irish driver, Pat Coldrick. We were taken to Saturday night "show off" events, like Mayfair at the Ritz Carlton, which was a "must attend" party for everybody who was anybody (or thought they were) in the then-current Broadway population.

Walter Winchell's one-paragraph rave had lifted us above obscurity to a position where we were being pointed out in a crowd. There was no question about the fact that we liked it.

Dorothy Davis spent time with Vilma, and Benny took me in tow during this preparation period before our debut at the Palace Theatre. Such an appearance was considered a mountain-peak of lifetime achievement for many veteran vaudeville performers—and here we were, starting there as featured dancers in Benny's *Broadway Stars of the Future*. Benny took me to all his familiar haunts: the Friars Club card room, handball courts, steam rooms, Lindy's restaurant, and of course, the old Madison Square Garden located then on Eighth Avenue and Forty-eighth Street.

Benny was truly like a father to me, showing me the ropes, introducing me to his friends, promoting Vilma and me at every opportunity, and seeing that we constantly met people of consequence everywhere.

His openhanded generosity and sponsorship was heartwarming, and he gave us a firm base of security in that often-terrifying monster of a city. These kindnesses we repaid later in service and loyalty. While other performers in his act left him at their first better offer, the Ebsens stayed on a second season and then left amicably to take their next step upward toward Broadway stardom, in the musical *Flying Colors*.

It was through Benny's efforts that I was sometimes positioned for chance contacts that were destined to relate mysteriously to my distant future.

Such was a night etched in my memory in the fall of 1930. The main boxing event at the "Garden" featured a colorful and flamboyant young heavyweight, just arrived from California in a convoy of Cadillacs containing friends, handlers

MAX BAER, SR. 1932

and retainers. (After having checked himself and his entourage into the Plaza, he had proceeded with his "training" at all the nightspots in town.) His opponent was to be Tom Heeney from New Zealand, once a great fighter but now a fading heavyweight.

Benny and I had seats at ringside in about the seventh row, and were enjoying the semifinals, when this tall, broad-shouldered young fighter, wearing a nondescript bathrobe, came down the aisle and eased himself into the vacant seat next to me. I don't remember that we exchanged a word, he being preoccupied with the action in the ring as he sat and alternately dealt the palm of either hand short, powerful jolts with his massive, taped fists. Later, with each blow these same fists literally disappeared into the "rubber-tired" fat of Tom Henney's midriff in a fight that lasted less than two rounds.

What Gypsy fortune teller could have told me that this devastating young slugger (who fought on to become the world's heavyweight champion) would one day father a son with whom I would eventually share world renown—in a yet-unknown communications medium, in a then-unwritten show. Or that this son, Max Baer, Jr., would one day use his great inherited strength and swift reflexes to save me from serious injury or death in an accident on the set while filming "The Beverly Hillbillies."

But I'm getting way ahead of my story.

CAPONE

In the fall of 1931, the Benny Davis act was playing the Oriental Theatre in Chicago. Benny had a sister who lived in Chicago, and I vaguely remember that she had something to do with Benny's association with the Capone organization.

Benny and the entire act were invited to a confirmation party for one of the mob's children, and on another occasion an invitation was extended for dinner at the Frolics nightclub. Vilma and I were not asked to the confirmation party, and Vilma was not asked to the Frolics due to Benny's fear that one of the hoodlums might be smitten with her and make unwanted advances. Then I would have to slug him, and there's no telling how an evening like that would end.

We arrived at the Frolics on the South Side about

AL CAPONE IN A PHOTOGRAPHER'S POSE.
ONE OF THE FIRST PORTRAITS OF THE FAMOUS "SCARFACE." 1932

11:00 P.M., after the last show at the Oriental. The room looked exactly like the nightclub ambience in any Cagney gangster movie set in the 1920s, except that these real characters seemed exaggerated.

There was heavy security sprinkled throughout the crowd: thick-necked, damaged-nose-and-ear types. In the left-upstage corner, two long rectangular tables were joined in an L-shape, with room to accommodate about twenty-four. Seated at the upstage table and pointed out to me were people with celebrated names like Anselmi, Jake Gusick and "Machine-gun" Jack McGurn. At the apex of the L, with his back to the wall, sat Al Capone. The table running downstage was occupied by Benny and us kids, as Capone's guests.

The dinner featured steak four inches thick; I found out years later that it was called *Chateaubriand*. It was superb and there was more than we could possibly eat, but we gave it a good try.

One at a time we were presented to our host, who smiled and shook hands without rising. Mr. Capone's hands were soft, like from not doing much gardening. The pupils of his eyes were so large, and their color merged so perfectly into the irises, that you found yourself looking into two pools of murky darkness. When he smiled I'm sure he intended it to be warm, but the effect was chilling. I felt like I was shaking hands with a smiling, scar-faced wolf!

During dinner, at the sound of an over-loud "Hey!" all the occupants of the two tables turned simultaneously to see that the "Hey" was addressed to Capone, and the voice came from a smallish, balding man with glasses, listing badly from a heavy load of "needled" beer.

Afterward, no one could figure out how this uninvited guest got there. But the tightest security does have lapses, especially when there's a nightclub floor show going on, and a line of girls is romping on and off stage right by Capone's table—within fanny-patting distance, that is.

The intruder's next line was accompanied by a shockingly familiar flip of his right hand onto Capone's left shoulder. "Are you Al Capone?" he challenged, slurring his words.

Instantly, two of Capone's guys had him. Capone, cool, and more amused than annoyed, gave an almost imperceptible sign, and the two men took their hands off. "Yeah," he said. "I'm Al Capone."

The little man's face beamed in sunny, inebriated affability.

"Well," he said, sticking out his paw, "I just wanna

BACKSTAGE AT THE EARLE THEATRE, PHILADELPHIA;
KIDDING AROUND WITH JIMMY DORSEY AND VILMA. 1934

shake your hand." Capone shook his hand, gave another sign to his henchmen, and the little man was whisked, not roughly, but efficiently, away.

Vilma was furious when she heard about all the fun she had missed, and thereafter she took to arranging her own social life.

When we played Rochester some weeks later, Vilma arranged a date with an attractive young college boy sporting a crew cut. His family happened to be in the business of importing olive oil. During the course of that evening, he opened up the store to show her around. During the tour, he casually spun around a display panel of fancy imported olives, revealing an arsenal of Thompson submachine guns concealed on the other side.

She one-upped us: Her steak at dinner that night was *five* inches thick. (And her date was a perfect host.)

That Vilma and I, two wholesome well-reared kids should meet and rub elbows with the grassroots beginnings of the Godfather set was not unusual for that time and place, the state of the nation, and the careers we had chosen. In nightclubs where the Davis act sometimes played, there was a definite overlapping of show business and the underworld.

Besides Capone, I met a stream of picturesque characters with names like "Cut-em-up Hymie," "Moon" Gambino, "Deuces" Frogly (whose mother made a world-class spaghetti sauce), and "Jewboy" Dietz; all outlaws—all generous hosts.

Any club worth playing was controlled by the local boss of illegal liquor traffic. These people were well-known and prospered through political connivance; they circulated freely in the Runyanesque world of Broadway, Lindy's, the racetracks, and the fringes of show business. They also survived, just as they do today, by supplying goods and services that a willing public will buy.

Today's "progressive society," however, has added one more facet to strengthen the sinews of underworld economics: drugs. In those days, drug traffic was nearly nonexistent and was considered by the majority of the mobs to be a dirty, disgusting and unrespectable business. Then, as talk-show hosts and their guests began doing marijuana jokes, and TV comedy shows did LSD sketches—with the laughter came acceptance.

"Doing" drugs became the smart, sophisticated "in" thing, creating a demand, a multibillion-dollar "take," and a worldwide scramble for a share of these dollars—a scramble, not excluding bankers.

The morality of it? Morality? What's that? How do you spell it? Oh, well, what the hell—everybody's doing it— so it must be OK.

So, now that the evil spirits of addiction plague the land, whence cometh the Merlin to re-stow them in Pandora's box?

Chapter 6

FLYING COLORS

In 1928, when Vilma and I were hoofing in Ziegfeld's *Whoopee*, alongside such international beauties as Gladys Glad, Ruby Keeler and Legs Diamond's girlfriend, Marion "Kiki" Roberts, the motion picture companies had a simple system for recruiting fresh Broadway talent. Each studio had a New York-based scout whose job it was to see every new show and send their bosses on the other coast an appraisal of the motion picture potential of any likely actor or actress.

Being human, these scouts were not infallible. One reported that Fred Astaire had: "No hair, no personality, dances a little."

Naturally, hopeful performers opening in a New York show looked forward with near-nauseating excitement to their crucial test. On this magical night would their years of

FLYING COLORS, THE FIRST MAJOR BROADWAY SUCCESS FOR VILMA AND ME. WE SCORED WITH THE NUMBER "WHEN THERE'S A SHINE ON YOUR SHOES." 1933

starvation and preparation be rewarded by the notice of a Hollywood scout? Would they be approached for a film test? Would the test be shipped to California and earn the nod of some film mogul? Would the test lead to a part in a picture, along with stardom, fame and riches?

The six years from 1928 to 1935 were Vilma's and my years of "starvation and preparation." They included the Ziegfeld chorus, two years of vaudeville and nightclubs with the Benny Davis act, *Broadway Stars of the Future*, which numbers among its graduates Martha Raye, Eleanor Powell, and the greatest natural dancer that ever hit Broadway—seventeen-year-old Hal Leroy.

Next came the Max Gordon show, *Flying Colors*. This was discovery time for us. Max Gordon, having achieved success with an intimate review starring Clifton Webb, Libby Holman and Fred Allen, figured he was on a roll and tried to do it again. This one starred Clifton Webb, Charlie Butterworth, Patsy Kelly and an exotic Russian ballet dancer, Tamara Geva, who was once married to George Balanchine. To insure his bet, Gordon decided to sprinkle in a little young, fresh talent. So he opened the door for the Ebsens. Our agent, Walter Batchelor, got us an audition with the show's writers, Howard Dietz and Arthur Schwartz.

We had just come from two seasons of hearing a big band's brass section blast out jazz for us to dance to. Now we were walking out onto the dark stage of a theater, handing our piano part to a rehearsal pianist we did not know, and trying to perform to an audience which consisted of reflections from two shining pairs of eyeglasses out there in the dark. There was no way we could be a sensation. We thought we had blown the audition until a phone call came from Batchelor. The news? Howard Dietz wanted to see us.

Apparently Dietz liked us, but he had reservations. Something about our name bothered him. He felt in order for us to achieve maximum success in his sophisticated revue, I would have to change my name to Buzz Kendall. I never heard what name he had in mind for Vilma, but I often wondered what magical turn my career would have taken had I complied with Howard's whim.

The show opened at the Forrest Theatre in Philadelphia. Vilma and I stopped it cold with a dance number called "When There's A Shine on Your Shoes." This created a problem. Clifton Webb screamed to the management that he, as the star, was not being protected, so our number was moved to every possible spot in the first act, hoping to diminish the audience response and thus quiet Webb's nerves. Wherever they put it, it stopped the show, so they returned it to where it was originally—in the seven spot— where it did the show the most good.

One night Clifton invited me into his dressing room and with all smiles and charm suggested he and I do a number together. I was flattered. Clifton never knew that while he was making his pitch to me, his campy black dresser— with whom his relationship was, at best, ambivalent—was voting his opinion with negative head shakes behind Clifton's back. The number never materialized.

Eventually the show opened at New York's Imperial Theatre, and suddenly we were the toast of Broadway. Walter Winchell titled his review, "Ebsens Make the Heart Grow Fonder," and playwright Noel Coward reportedly said, "The Ebsens are sheer bliss."

Years later, Tennessee Williams eloquently described

the experience of "arriving." He wrote, "After years of clawing your way forward by your fingernails across a glazed surface, you arrive at the door which bars your way. You rise and lean your shoulder against it. The door gives way so easily you fall headlong into the next room."

So it felt to us. Suddenly all doors were open to us. We could do no wrong. We were feeling the sweet, heady, intoxicating thrill of success. No champagne can touch it. *Flying Colors* was great for us, and when it closed we took off for the French Riviera, worked the Sporting De'te in Monte Carlo for the summer, and returned to New York to a featured spot in the *Ziegfeld Follies of 1934*. Actually, the show was produced by the Shuberts, who had purchased the name from Flo Ziegfeld's widow, actress Billie Burke. (Billie later played Glinda the Good Witch in the film, *The Wizard of Oz*.)

Ziegfeld Follies starred Fanny Brice and Willie and Eugene Howard. Vilma and I were featured dancers in this standard Broadway revue with singing, dancing, comedy sketches and a chorus line. The score was by Yip Harburg and Vernon Duke.

We stopped the show on opening night in Boston with "I Like the Likes of You." We sang one chorus and danced a simple, easy little soft-shoe number. The audience ate it up.

Disregarding the ancient truism "If it ain't broke, don't fix it," the creative brains of the show pounced on this morsel of success in an otherwise spotty program and decided to beef it up by adding four choruses of "production." Our number never again stopped the show. I learned two lessons. First, never let anyone mess around with something that's working for you. And second, if you encounter a serious problem while performing and can't ad-lib your way out of it, let the audience in on it. The latter was executed beautifully and with great success opening night in New York.

Fanny Brice's throat closed up during her big comedy song. She finally stopped trying to sing, looked at the audience, shrugged with a helpless gesture, and said, "It *would* happen to me on opening night." The audience gave her a heartwarming ovation, which relaxed her. Her singing voice came back, and she finished the number to solid applause.

Some years later, I had a chance to employ Fanny's lesson while playing *The Male Animal* in a summer theater production in Great Neck, Long Island. At one point in the play, an actor was supposed to say to me, "Turner, I've just got one thing to say to you. You read that letter today and you're out of this university tomorrow."

Well, he got as far as "I've got just one thing to say to you . . ." and then just stood there with his mouth open and panic in his eyes. He could *not* think of the next line. Finally, he turned on his heel and walked off the stage. I looked longingly after him as he exited. Then I took two steps in the other direction—looked back at the door—no actor—so I turned to the audience and said, "Well, I can always do a soft-shoe dance." The audience, having sensed the situation, burst into laughter and applause. The actor, having checked the line, sheepishly re-entered, crossed to me and we finished the scene.

Strangely coincidental, the identical problem occurred the following week with another actor in another city. This time I was ready for him. When he drew the mental blank, I simply said, "I suppose you're going to tell me that if I read that letter today, I'll be out of this university tomorrow." The actor blinked—said, "Yeah," and the show went on.

During these active years, Vilma and I were approached by scouts from all the major film companies: Warner Bros., RKO, Paramount. But we had a prudent New York lawyer named Howard Reinheimer who had a strong belief that was anathema to Hollywood—that its actor-procurement formula known as the "seven plus seven" deal was unjust. Simply, this standard contract for a newcomer guaranteed only six months' employment while committing the actor to another thirteen-and-a-half years in six-month option increments. The initial salary and the raise, in most cases, was $250 in each period. Many performers jumped at those deals since it never occurred to them that the option would not be picked up. A lot of them thought: With my talent, all I need is to get in front of those cameras and the world is mine. Give me the pen. Where do I sign? Of course, an actor is nothing without confidence!

Studios were always pleased to see actors splurge, buy houses, boats, and expensive cars. Then, if the studio wanted to chisel—that is, offer to pick up the option, minus the raise—the actor would be so heavily mortgaged he would be easy to deal with. Of course, if all went well, by the end of the fourteen years—if he lived that long—the actor could be earning $3,500, which was a lot of money in the late-20s and early-30s. This was tempting to anyone riding the crest of a series of New York flops—or even successes with those dispiriting layoffs in between.

The system worked fine for any actor of modest

potential, but what if he or she became an instant blockbusting star like Jimmy Cagney, who was a former New York "Gypsy" (chorus boy). Cagney's pictures were making millions for the Warner brothers, and he hadn't even worked out his first seven years. After that, the studio had him for another seven years. That's when the big money started, they informed you. There'd be sweet talk of altered contracts and bonuses. But what if you burned out before then, and nobody wanted you anymore? The system bred discontent, walkouts and blacklisting. Hollywood was a company town of many companies and bitter rivals—until they were threatened. Then they closed ranks. If an actor became troublesome, he was blacklisted.

Our lawyer, Howard Reinheimer, had logged many hours of negotiation with Hollywood studios on behalf of such clients as Oscar Hammerstein, Jerome Kern, Irving Berlin, George Kaufman and Maxwell Anderson. Let's just say he handled the cream of the New York creative talent. He was secure. The threat of being "barred from the lot," a weapon the studios effectively used against Hollywood-based negotiators, did not intimidate Reinheimer. His clients didn't need Hollywood. They had someplace else to go. They had Broadway. But now that the movies had learned to talk, Hollywood needed their product. So Howard could negotiate with what the Hollywood producers felt was impudent independence. They hated him—a fact he found amusing.

I think the deal he devised for Vilma and me, he did partly for his own entertainment. We certainly couldn't pay much, and he knew it. His annual fee the first few years was $200. He always seemed embarrassed and reluctant to bill us.

We met Howard through Vilma's husband, Bobby Dolan, a volatile and engaging young Irishman from Montreal. Bobby, or Robert Emmett Dolan as he was later known when he achieved status as a conductor and producer, was the pit piano player in *Flying Colors*. Bobby was Broadway- and Hollywood-wise. He had done a stint at Warner Bros. as a songwriter with lyricist and fellow Irishman Walter O'Keefe when he was so young his father had to sign his contract. He impetuously fell in love with Vilma during rehearsals and charmed her out of her engagement to a stable Philadelphia newspaperman, Nelson Hesse. Vilma was bedazzled by Bobby's dinners at "21" and introductions to the glamorous Algonquin Set, of which Bobby was a young darling. After a whirlwind courtship, they were married. Bobby was an extremely capable musician. He was also a good man to have on your side in a contest of

ON THE SET WITH DIRECTOR ROY DEL RUTH AND SID SILVERS IN
BORN TO DANCE. 1937

connivance. Let the following scenario attest:

When Bobby got a job in California as a musical conductor for the Burns and Allen radio show, his first thought after settling in was: How do I get my wife out here? Oscar Hammerstein and Jerome Kern (friends of Bobby's) were under contract at the MGM lot and assigned to write a musical with a collegiate background. Upon arrival, Bobby called Oscar and was invited to dinner. Days later, Robert Rubin, an MGM vice president who ran the New York office, received an *urgent* request from the West Coast to "test the Ebsens."

These instructions were passed on to Rubin's assistant, Billy Grady, who contacted our agent Walter Batchelor, who then contacted us. It was December, 1934, and Vilma and I were playing the Central Park Casino. The club's land and the building were owned by the city, and since the pop-

BIG PRODUCTION NUMBER FROM *BORN TO DANCE.* 1937

ular and debonair Jimmy Walker "owned" the city, the Casino became his personal nightclub. It was franchised (under terms which will probably never become full public knowledge) to a gentleman named Sidney Soloman, who was well-known in the trade as "slow-pay." An additional negative was low-pay, but the real payoff was prestige.

Since I have played bucolic characters so long and so convincingly, people tend to perceive me as a country yokel with hayseeds in my hair. Yet my last job in New York before moving to Hollywood was dancing at the Casino, the city's swankiest nightclub. There, in faultless evening attire—for me that meant a hat, white tie and tails, and for Vilma a Bonwit Teller evening dress—we entertained the super *haute monde* in New York's most legendary, prestigious and exclusive nightclub.

Vilma and I worked there for $150 a week. Our next job was in Hollywood at $1,500 a week. This miracle was a tribute to the negotiating skills, the conniving and the finesse of the people on our team. The salary advance was, of course, a big score, but what made the deal absolutely unheard-of in 1934 was the length of the contract. Two years, with a two-year option.

Billy Grady had been responsible for getting our signatures on an optional standard contract *before* the screen test was made. But in the face of frantic demands for the Ebsens from the West Coast (Hammerstein and Kern were tugging from within) and our strategic elusiveness (playing dates out of town), Grady had no one to talk to but Reinheimer and Walter Batchelor, who maintained a united front. "Two years or nothing," they repeated like a broken record. Poor Billy Grady was being whipsawed.

LEAPING FOR JOY IN *BORN TO DANCE*. 1937

We caught the Twentieth Century for Chicago in the same train station where I had arrived six years earlier with $26.65. We were headed for Hollywood. Actor's heaven.

I kept thinking how thrilled and proud our folks would be. Our father, who taught us *his* trade—dancing. Our mother, who encouraged us through every roadblock, every setback and every temporary defeat. Our sister Norma, who staked me to the $50 that took me to New York. Our sister Helga, who like another little mother, helped raise us. I thought of Leslie, the youngest one who didn't live. I kept thinking that she, too, would have been proud.

The night seemed to fly by as we clickety-clacked through towns we had played with the Benny Davis act, *Broadway Stars of the Future*. And here we were, living the title. Rochester, Syracuse, Detroit and Toledo all flew by. I slept very little and didn't miss it. Sustained euphoria.

A SCENE FROM *BANJO ON MY KNEE* STARRING BARBARA STANWYCK, JOEL MC CREA, WALTER BRENNAN AND KATHERINE DE MILLE. 1937

Chicago meant a change to the Superchief. We had a four-hour layover, and since our baggage was checked through we strolled State Street, "that great street," replaying memories: the Oriental Theatre, the Occidental Restaurant, the Chicago, the College Inn, the State and Lake where we had played five shows a day with Benny, all the while learning audiences. Taking them in stride. The warm ones, the cold ones, the sparse ones. Pacing, seasoning, maturing, learning how to perform. And I never forgot Benny admonishing: "Never let down. Work just as hard at a supper show for a mere handful. You never know who might be out there. Don't be annoyed at a small house. Don't be mad at the ones who do come. Give 'em their money's worth." The fundamentals of show business we had learned from Benny Davis were now paying off. We were another step up the ladder.

WITH BARBARA STANWYCK,
ONE OF MY FAVORITE DANCING PARTNERS. 1937

Vilma's husband, Bobby, had informed us that no one of any consequence arrived in California on anything but the Superchief, and only the most *gauche* peasant rode this posh Santa Fe carrier all the way to Union Station in downtown Los Angeles. It was "in" to get off in Pasadena, and Bobby was there to greet us.

I will never forget the skin-caressing balminess reminiscent of Florida, that first look, smell and feel of California. It was truly the Golden State. Golden hills, golden oranges, golden sunshine and golden salaries. There was no smog then and the distant snowcapped mountains stood out in the clear, crystal air. The people were friendly, dressed in attractive summer clothes; it was so different from the

THREE REMORSEFUL JAILBIRDS AFTER A BRAWL IN *BANJO ON MY KNEE.*
WALTER BRENNAN, JOEL MC CREA AND ME. 1937

February we had left behind in New York.

We spent the first night in the Knickerbocker Hotel on Ivar Street. In 1934 it was quite a respectable place to stay while you were looking for a residence. Bobby had found a house on Wyton Drive in Westwood, where we were soon ensconced in a *ménage*, consisting of Vilma, Bobby, his arranger Herbie Spencer, me, and a cook named Matthew who loved to fish from "all-day boats" (a nightmarish recreation he introduced to Vilma and me—it haunts me still).

Not wishing to risk breaching any aspect of our contract, I suggested to Bobby that we report to the studio immediately. He laughed at me. "This is Hollywood," he said. "They have your number. When they want you, they'll call you." And then he left to do his musical chores for the Burns and Allen Show. He sounded confident and reasonable, but I worried. Fifteen hundred dollars a week was more money than we had ever been associated with, so after consulting with Vilma, we had Matthew drive us over to the studio.

On a sprawling 300 acres fronting on Washington Boulevard in Culver City stood Metro-Goldwyn-Mayer Studios. It was so big that it was divided into three lots. Lot One contained fifteen sound stages, the administration office, buildings that housed creative talent, dressing rooms, wardrobe, properties, the commissary and a gymnasium. Atop the tallest sound stage was a huge electric sign of the MGM logo which featured a roaring Leo the Lion, king of the jungle. The commanding visage of Leo was said by some to have been inspired by the spirit of Louis B. Mayer, the absolute boss of this studio and acknowledged King of the Hollywood Jungle. Lot Two, or "the back lot," contained

permanent outdoor location backgrounds and a vast tank. Lot Three had more of the same.

We cruised the length of the frontage on Washington, looking for a breach in the walls. At the very eastern end next to a narrow iron-gated sally port with a security guard was a door marked "Casting." This might be it.

Instructing Matthew to park somewhere and stand by, Vilma and I went through the door and found ourselves in a nine-by-twelve-foot undecorated room. There was a bench against one wall, and a door in the upper right-hand corner that was buzzer-controlled by its guardian, a gum-smacking blonde spiritually akin to radio's Myrt and Marge. A handful of people stood in line. Extras or bit players, I figured. They held brief conversations with the keeper of the gate.

"We're the Ebsens," I said when it came our turn. I gave her the warm, friendly smile that had always worked for me in New York. Her face was stone.

"So?" she said.

"We work here," Vilma volunteered, friendly as a basket full of kittens.

The inner sanctum's keeper just stared. "Have a seat."

We went back to the bench while she had an unintelligible phone conversation, eyeing us. A parade of newcomers took over her attention.

Twenty minutes later we were still on the bench. I got up again and approached her. She looked at me blankly. "We're the Ebsens," I said again. "We have a contract to work here."

"For who?" she asked.

"MGM," I said.

She nodded with a hint of annoyance. "Any particular

producer?"

"Oscar Hammerstein," I chanced.

She consulted her typed list. "Mr. Hammerstein has checked off the lot." Verbally, she didn't add "you fraud," but her eyes did.

We began to see the wisdom of Bobby's advice and left. We relaxed and began to enjoy California. We found out later that Oscar Hammerstein had completed his assignment and moved on. A brand-new producer, Sam Katz, unknown even to the secretaries and gatekeepers had inherited us; but still we weren't on the lot.

One day we got a frantic call from Sam Katz's secretary. The message was, in effect, "Where the hell have you been? We've been looking all over for you."

"Trying to get into the studio," I told them.

They sent a limousine for us.

VILMA, ELEANOR POWELL AND ME IN *BROADWAY MELODY OF 1936*.
NOTE THE MICKEY MOUSE SWEATER—THE FIRST!

BROADWAY MELODY

Sam Katz and his partner Barney Balaban owned and operated a chain of movie theaters in the Midwest.

With straight vaudeville houses a thing of the past, there was still enough public demand for live entertainment to justify production of one-hour stage presentations to play their circuit in conjunction with the movie.

Thus, for 65¢ (until 6:00 P.M. when the price doubled) the public could enjoy three hours of diversified entertainment: a movie and a stage show. With four audience turnovers daily, the Balaban and Katz theaters were doing well.

But Katz was ambitious.

He had an idea. Why not take the successful stage presentation formula, expand it to two hours, hold it together with a simple love story and make it into a moving picture?

And that is what set Sam's course toward Hollywood, where he emerged as the new Wizard on the lot at the Metro-Goldwyn-Mayer Studio.

Since he was not the nephew of any reigning Wizard, the rumor was that he "bought in" with Loews, Inc. stock.

At any rate, he was the producer who inherited the Ebsens, and the story he selected as a framework for his idea was a remake of the MGM success *Broadway Melody of 1929*, a musical feature film starring Charlie King, Bessie Love and Cliff Edwards.

The result became the smashing *Broadway Melody of 1936*, populated by solid vaudeville-bred performers Jack Benny, Sid Silvers, June Knight, Eleanor Powell, Nick Long, Jr., and us.

The only non-vaudeville graduate was the male love

interest, ultra-handsome and budding young movie heart-throb, Robert Taylor.

The song number assigned to Vilma and me was "Sing Before Breakfast." And mindful of our competition, we set about making it a world-beater.

We threw out all our old easy steps and substituted flashier ones, "over the tops," "wings," "trenches," and multi-tap combinations we had never even tried before. In our determination to be a success, we rehearsed till our legs gave out. We thought we were great!

The letdown came at the first choreography run-through.

We performed in the rehearsal hall for a group of assembled "brass," a tough jury composed of producer, director, cameraman, assorted executives and their yes men, so we really gave it everything we had.

Our performance was greeted by a thudding, embarrassing silence.

We were shattered.

Before he left the room, Sam Katz took us aside. "Kids," he said, "what you did was not bad. It was just disappointing. It would be OK for audiences that paid sixty-five cents to get in, but because of your background in top Broadway musicals, we expect "six-sixty" material from you. Now, why don't you try again?"

That night Vilma and I did a lot of thinking. Her husband, Bobby Dolan, joined us in the rap session.

What came out of it were two conclusions: first, a musical number ideally should move the story along, and second—use the props.

In the set for the number, "Sing Before Breakfast,"

there was one obvious prop—the coffee pot! Like a light bulb snapping on in our heads, the thought came to us simultaneously—we coax the stubborn pot into perking, at first intermittently, then puffing steam on the beat by the rhythm of our feet and the beat of the music.

Besides our rehearsal pianist and our prop man, it took a portable steam boiler and a special-effects crew of three to work it, plus a man with a sense of rhythm to properly time and release the puffs of steam.

We rehearsed for a week, and this time the "jury" loved it, the audiences in the theaters loved it, and the *New York Times* movie critic singled it out as the one touch in the picture that suggested the creative imagination of the renowned French director, René Claire.

Soon after our successful debut in *Broadway Melody* of

LOCAL BOY MAKES GOOD. WELCOMED HOME TO ORLANDO
BY MAYOR DELANEY WAY. 1937

1936, MGM found the one flaw in Howard Reinheimer's contract. By its terms there was nothing to prevent the studio from separating us as a team, and that is what they did.

It was a traumatic time of tears and heartaches, but it did prolong Vilma's marriage to Bobby because she went back to New York with him and, like a good wife, helped him become Broadway's pre-eminent pit conductor and later a Hollywood producer. She even found time, before starting a family, to further her own career in a show with London dancing star Jack Buchanan.

Meanwhile, back in Oz, my option had been picked up, and I proceeded to serve out my contract.

CAST OF *BROADWAY MELODY OF 1938*.
FRONT ROW LEFT TO RIGHT: JUDY GARLAND, SOPHIE TUCKER, ELEANOR POWELL AND
HARRIET PARSONS (LOUELLA'S DAUGHTER). BACK ROW LEFT TO RIGHT: IGOR GORIN,
BILLY GILBERT, GEORGE MURPHY, ME AND ROBERT TAYLOR. (SEE CHAPTER 9)

Chapter 8

SHIRLEY TEMPLE

Of all the moppet stars to come down the pike, the most classic, enduring, and once-in-a-lifetime package of talent and stardom was Shirley Temple.

Out of the Meglin Kiddie School of child theatrical trainees came a horde of what sophisticated deadpan comedian Charlie Butterworth used to call "little monsters." These kids could tap dance like machine-gun fire and belt your eardrums with an embarrassingly adult song while doing a Mae West imitation. Driven by their mothers, a confrontation with a roomful of these wound-up and turned-on little dolls was traumatic. Butterworth had a standing offer: a bounty of $5 for the head of a Meglin Kiddie, a sardonic joke repeated with hilarity among the transplanted Algonquin set in which Charlie moved.

SHIRLEY TEMPLE BECAME MY LITTLEST DANCING PARTNER IN
CAPTAIN JANUARY STARRING GUY KIBBEE, SLIM SUMMERVILLE AND JUNE LANG.
ONE OF SHIRLEY'S MOST SUCCESSFUL FILMS. 1937

For some of these youngsters, who were victims of ambitious parents, the experience was tragic if they were not meant to be performers. But some were, and of these the most fetching, the most captivating, the most talented, was Shirley. She had a voice that had in it the quality of breaking dawn. In *Baby Take a Bow*, a mediocre picture, she did a number with Jimmy Dunn and the house came down, and Twentieth Century-Fox stock went up. At Twentieth, they knew exactly what to do with her. After a loan-out to Paramount for *Little Miss Marker*, her pictures were paying the freight for the entire studio. Behind her back, Shirley's mother was known as "the goose that laid the golden egg," but to her face, she was treated with respectful reverence. Mrs. Temple was a no-nonsense and formidable woman.

When I was making 1936's *Captain January*, I marveled that director Dave Butler and producer Buddy DeSylva allowed me to pick Shirley up and dance with her over some bales and barrels on a dock in the Codfish Ball number. The worried look on the men's faces told me what I already knew. I was holding the principal assets of Twentieth Century-Fox in my arms, and I had better not drop her.

Shirley's days began at 4:00 A.M. She was allowed an hour and a half for dressing and breakfast, followed by a half-hour ride to the studio, which was spent learning the lines for the day's shooting. And little Shirley didn't just learn her own lines. It seemed easier for her to learn *everyone's* lines, which led to difficulties. Sometimes it was necessary to cut to Shirley for a reaction while the other actor in the scene was speaking. Sometimes, the camera caught her lips moving as she silently mouthed the line along with him.

Since the California courts and the Board of Education are uncompromising in the matter of schooling for theatrical children, when there is a child working on a set there is always a teacher present. For approximately every hour Shirley appeared before the camera, she spent an hour with the teacher. This called for strict budgeting of Shirley's time, and a shooting schedule tailored to accommodate these educational statutes. My own problem was that, having been loaned by MGM to Twentieth Century-Fox to do a song and dance with Shirley Temple, I could not get a moment of her time to frame the number.

My choreographer Jack Donohue (not the Broadway star) whom I had brought in for the job, was frustrated, and I was worried. There was so much to do and so little time to do it. Eddie Powell, the arranger, was dunning us for the musical routine. The number had to be scored and prerecorded. The prop department was standing by, and the rehearsal pianist was aimlessly noodling away the day; it was stress-making. I knew that one day the director, the producers, the cameramen, and all of their minions would walk in and say, "We shoot this number tomorrow. Let's see it"—and there would be no number to be seen! One day I laid out the problem, forcefully, for the unit manager.

Next morning at 9:00 A.M. there walked into the Hall of Music, our rehearsal hall, a Meglin Kiddie. A "dance-in" (versus a stand-in). She was no Shirley Temple, but she was willing and she could move, and her mother was reasonably quiet. We went to work and in three days we had the semblance of a number—rough, but a good start. Then, of course, before we could do any more we had to teach it to Shirley. Somehow we were allowed to steal her from the set

DANCING WITH SHIRLEY TEMPLE WAS HARD ON THE KNEES
UNTIL WE BROUGHT HER UP IN THE WORLD. 1937

(ABOVE) A TENSE MOMENT IN *CAPTAIN JANUARY*. 1937

(BELOW) A MORE RELAXED MOMENT: A LITTLE HULA AND SOME MUSIC. 1937

for fifteen minutes.

Accompanied by an assistant director, Shirley arrived in a limousine, came in, sat down, and we did the number for her. I asked if she liked it and she said yes. Then, since we had her there and weren't sure when we might see her again, I suggested she get up and learn the routine. And that was when I got a lesson in professionalism from a six-year old.

"Is it set?" Shirley said, without moving a muscle.

"Well, no . . . " I stammered. "We might make some changes."

"Let me know when it's set and I'll learn it," she said, and trailing her assistant director, out the door she went into her waiting limo to be driven back to the set. For a brief moment, I wanted to paddle her.

Jack and I exchanged wry grins. Since our chorus days on Broadway, we had been "handled" by people in power, but never by a six-year old. What staved off our anger was that there was no hint of "spoiled brat" conceit in what she had done. She was merely saving energy. She was holding down an adult's job, working long hours, learning lines and lyrics and performing them flawlessly, besides learning the three R's: reading, 'riting and 'rithmetic. Once I saw her host a table of Mexican dignitaries and their families at lunch. Keeping everyone smiling and the conversation going, she had the aplomb of a matron.

Jack and I and the dance-in Meglin Kiddie wasted no time in getting the routine set, and Shirley came in and learned it in two half-hour sessions. We shot it on the wharf set located on the back lot approximately where the pool of Century City's Century Plaza Hotel exists today. The number

CAPTAIN JANUARY. 1936

was a smashing success. In fact, it's probably played more times and viewed by more people than any musical number Shirley ever did. Years later, in her autobiography, Shirley labeled me her best dancing partner, a compliment I'll never forget.

Shirley is an American phenomenon whose legend is self-perpetuating. She went on to modest success as an ingenue and adult actress but served best and gained career renown as a diplomatic envoy to Ghana and Czechoslovakia.

After the last day of shooting *Captain January* with her, I didn't see Shirley for some thirty-five years. At a testimonial dinner for her in the Twentieth Century-Fox commissary, I walked in and began greeting friends. Suddenly I heard a familiar voice coming from an area where cameras and flashbulbs were clicking and popping.

"Hi, Buddy!"

I looked in the direction of the voice. An attractive, smiling woman gave me the clue.

"It's *me* —Shirley!"

We hugged and I was glad to see her, but as we embraced an irreverent thought surfaced—I love you, Shirley, but I'm glad I don't have to lift and carry you over those boxes and barrels today. I don't think I could make it.

SHIRLEY TEMPLE BLACK GRADUATED TO A CAREER IN INTERNATIONAL POLITICS. 1982

Chapter 9

OZ

One of the first people I met on the Metro-Goldwyn-Mayer lot was Arthur Freed. Arthur fully fit the meaning of "ubiquitous." I was constantly encountering him: in the commissary, on the way to a sound stage, in a recording session, or on the way to a projection room. But where you would find him most frequently was close to the boss of the studio, L.B. Mayer.

Whenever Mr. Mayer found it necessary to walk from one side of the lot to another, he could be sure of a loyal volunteer escort in Arthur Freed, who usually took a position abreast of him. Freed attentively listened and nodded in agreement and was always tactfully ready to drop a respectful pace behind, but not out of earshot should Mayer encounter someone he wished to speak with privately along

YOUNG JUDY GARLAND WAS A HEART-STEALER AND A CHARMING PROFESSIONAL IN THE FILM THAT LAUNCHED HER INTO STARDOM, *BROADWAY MELODY OF 1938*.

the way. So familiar was this sight that some stag-roast wag is credited with the remark, "If you kicked L.B. Mayer in the ass, Arthur Freed would get a bloody nose."

Criticism of someone's *modus operandi* sometimes becomes less valid when measured against results, and for Arthur Freed the results were fantastic. He rose from lyrics writer to a position of power on the lot, having to his credit the production of some of the most successful pictures MGM ever made.

But Freed had been programmed as a winner in L.B.'s mind very early in the game. In Mayer's box at Santa Anita racetrack, Arthur invariably held the winning ticket. Of course there were those jealous detractors who said he bet on every horse in the race, but again, consider the results. He got the job, and his pictures all made money.

Arthur seemed to like me, and I was glad of it. One day Arthur walked into the rehearsal hall on the lot, shepherding a cute, long-legged thirteen-year old.

"Meet your new dancing partner," he said.

This was my introduction to Judy Garland. Judy was the youngest member of a singing act known as the Gumm Sisters, which an unsentimental MGM split up, just as they had separated Vilma and me.

Judy was an instantaneous smash in her first picture, *Broadway Melody of 1938*, a film we worked in together. She was the bobbysoxer who sang "You Made Me Love You" to a fan picture of Clark Gable. I taught her the little shimsham-shimmy number, which we did together in the finale. Judy showed great promise, but the creative brains on the lot did not yet know what to do with her.

When plans for a production of *The Wizard of Oz* were

discussed many months later, word trickled down that another of my motion picture dancing partners, Shirley Temple, was the choice for Dorothy Gale, the young farm girl who spins into a Technicolor dream and lands in a place called Oz.

That deal fell through, and Judy Garland was selected for the part. In retrospect, MGM stockholders never got a better break; although Shirley would have been charming, her studio, Twentieth Century-Fox, would have wanted an arm and a leg to lend her to another studio. And songs such as "Over the Rainbow" got a belting ride from Judy Garland that Shirley's cute vocal equipment could not have delivered.

Arthur Freed approached me one day with a twinkle in his eye. I could tell he had good news and was elated to be the bearer. He had just come from a high-level production meeting and was twitching to leak a morsel of news. People love to deliver good news, especially in the world of show business where there is a tendency to associate the messenger with the happy memory. There is no telling how high the recipients will go or how powerful they may become, so the memory could pay dividends for the bearer downstream. On the other hand, bad news—like an option not being picked up—is something you don't hear about until the gate man halts your entrance to the studio, or you find your parking space reassigned.

"Guess who is going to play the Scarecrow in *The Wizard of Oz*?" he asked me. "You!"

It was wonderful news. I had known the book as a child but was not a particular aficionado of its creator L. Frank Baum and his "further adventures with *Oz*" books, silent films, and such. The big draw for me was that the movie was to be produced in *color*. *Oz* was to be one of the studio's biggies, and I was to have an important part. Maybe the most important in my life as an actor. It meant prestige, a building of my career, and a practical guarantee they would want me to stay on beyond my brief two-year deal, which portended juicy negotiations and fat profits on the next contract go-around. An actor is nothing without a part to play. Just the anticipation can send him into the upper realms of a pink cloud of euphoria. I shared the good news with my wife, my friends, my agent Walter Batchelor in New York, and my parents. It was a time I'll always remember. I rushed to the rehearsal hall and began plotting my Scarecrow dances and wobbles.

That's where I was when Ray Bolger walked in with his agent, Abe Lastfogel. I had known Ray slightly from New York. He was a superb comic dancer and he had headlined in clubs and in vaudeville. He did a falling-down dance which was hilarious, just the kind of routine, it suddenly occurred to me, that would be the perfect Scarecrow dance. That's when those icy fingers started running down my spine.

Ray's agent, Abe, grinned into my stricken face and said, "Ray's going to play the Scarecrow in *The Wizard of Oz*." I knew it for the truth. Abe Lastfogel *was* the William Morris office, and the William Morris office was all-powerful.

Arthur Freed didn't want to be labeled the "trouble-making blabbermouth," so he quickly grabbed me, fearful that I would walk into someone's office and start screaming that I had been promised the Scarecrow part. "Look, I'm just a buck private around here," he told me. His face was deadly serious, and he said, "Whatever you do, don't tell anybody that I said you were going to play the Scarecrow. Ray is going to be the Scarecrow." Then, with what seemed like remarkable daring, he blurted out, "You're going to play the Tin Woodman!"

Soon after, I received official confirmation, and I became determined to make the role of the Tin Woodman a winner.

What followed was an all-out program of research and development of a viable costume and makeup for the Tin Woodman. I was the guinea pig. A consortium of brains from the wardrobe and prop departments, assuming that tin meant tin, made me a suit out of stovepipe. The experience verified my belief that there is very little stretch in stovepipe. I put it on. The suit had primitive knee- and arm-bending accommodations—like a suit of armor. The torso covering worked, but the crotch area had very sharp edges. One leg disputed the other with such noisy metal-clashing it made me nervous.

"Walk," someone said. I walked, and I sounded like a junk wagon going down a bumpy road.

"Dance," someone said.

I did a time-step—very carefully. It sounded like two junk wagons in a chariot race.

"Open up! Broaden your movements," a voice prompted.

I did a hitch-kick and almost gave myself an ad lib sex change. I yelled in pain and explained the problem to a sympathetic Richard Thorpe, the director. He ordered, "Get

him out of there! The part doesn't call for a soprano."

The second model of the Tin Man suit was an improvement. It was essentially the same construction, but it was created of stiff cardboard covered with a silvery, metallic-looking paper. It was lighter, quieter, and cut so it was less hazardous to the occupant. I wish I could say as much for the makeup.

The high priest of the MGM makeup department was Jack Dawn. He had reigned there for years, his suzerainty unchallenged, supported by miracles he had accomplished in filling the cracks and disguising the blemishes of many world-famous faces including those of Joan Crawford, Norma Shearer, and Greta Garbo. Dawn did a fine creative job on

WITH BERT LAHR AND RAY BOLGER DURING THE FIRST TEN DAYS OF
SHOOTING MGM'S *THE WIZARD OF OZ.* 1939

Bolger as the Scarecrow and Bert Lahr as the Cowardly Lion. With me, he made just one mistake—nearly fatal.

There were many unexplainable delays in the film's production, then by late September of 1938 we began weeks of rehearsal. The filming started in October. The makeup call for me was 6:00 A.M. I had time for a quick cup of coffee, then came the application of a very thin rubber cap to cover my hair and make my head into a knob. Next, a molded rubber nose was glued on to simulate an oilcan spout, and that was followed with a molded rubber chin with rivets to suggest the assemblage of this mechanical man. After the false pieces were applied, a coat of clown-white grease paint was smeared over my entire head and neck area. Next came the giant step in the wrong direction: The makeup people powdered their entire creation with aluminum dust.

The whole apparatus was torture. The modified tin suit was improved but still it was no joy. It was almost impossible to sit down. To dance was an ordeal of pain, yet somehow I got through six weeks of rehearsal in it. When we shot scenes in full makeup and costume under blazing lights, I sweated. The makeup ran, and the camera operator complained that the clown-white was showing through, so the makeup man, armed with a huge powder puff, continuously applied fresh clouds of aluminum dust to my face. It was impossible not to breathe the stuff.

Bert and Ray were complaining, too, about the difficulty and discomfort of their costumes and makeup. Much of the time on the set was spent cooling off the actors and attempting to relieve us in some way as we shot out-of-sequence scenes from the witch's castle to the Yellow Brick Road.

For some mysterious reason, reports on the "rushes" (film that had been shot the day before) were strangely nonexistent. If anybody had seen them, they weren't talking, and this included the director, Richard Thorpe, a quiet-spoken, sensitive gentleman whose concentration and deep concern with today's problems did not invite discussion of yesterday's.

Finally, the quiet was broken. A summons from on high. The company was shut down. The principal actors, Bert, Ray, Judy and myself, were to report to our producer Mervyn LeRoy at 10:00 A.M. the following morning. No excuses. We looked at each other. What could this mean?

Mervyn was a small man, sitting behind a large desk, chewing a large cigar. As we assembled, he acknowledged our presence with a nod, a terse greeting, and a chilly look. Then, without much preamble, he launched into an individual and then collective chewing out the likes of which I have never experienced in all my years of show business. It was as virulent as it was unjustified, and as I listened my own anger mounted. It was insulting.

I remember him yelling, "I don't know what the hell you people are doing out there! It looks like ladies' night in a Turkish bath!" I figured he must've been the recipient of a chewing out from L.B. Mayer, and he was passing it on to us. When in doubt, whip the actors. Make 'em act better.

He went on along those lines, and we sat there stunned. To the best of our abilities, we were doing what we were told to do and what we were directed to do and what the lines called for. We hadn't seen the rushes, but if they looked bad, we had no control of that.

At one point LeRoy paused for a breath, reached for a fresh two-dollar cigar, bit off the end and lit it. From the time I entered the room, I had been fascinated by his cigar holder. It was an eye-catching focal point: an elephant's foot fashioned into a humidor. It was obscene.

Poor goddamn elephant, I kept thinking. Had to die so this little bastard could have a place to keep his cigars.

It was several days later when my cramps began. My first symptoms had been a noticeable shortness of breath. I would breathe and exhale and then get the panicky feeling I hadn't breathed at all. Then I would gasp for another quick breath with the same result. My fingers began to cramp, and then my toes. For a time I could control this unusual cramping by forcibly straightening out my fingers and toes.

One night in bed I woke up screaming. My arms were cramping from my fingers upward and curling simultaneously so that I could not use one arm to uncurl the other. My wife tried to pull my arm straight with some success, just as my toes began to curl; then my feet and legs bent backward at the knees. I panicked. What was happening to me? Next came the worst. The cramps in my arms advanced into my chest to the muscles that controlled my breathing. If this continued, I wouldn't even be able to take a breath. I was sure I was dying.

"Call Dave," I gasped out the words. Dave Baird was my sailing companion, and he lived nearby. My wife called him and an ambulance, and they arrived simultaneously. Twenty minutes later, strapped to a gurney and breathing from an oxygen tank, I listened to the siren and watched the lights of Wilshire Boulevard blur by on our way to the Good Samaritan Hospital. Dave was seated beside me, holding my hand. Then I fell asleep.

I woke up confused, lying under a small Plexiglass tent, which covered my chest and head. From the sunshine in the window, I figured it was morning. In the distance, I heard the nurse answering the phone.

"Milton who?" she said. "Milton LeRoy?"

Mervyn LeRoy. How nice of him to call. My benign thoughts were dashed with her next lines. She was Irish and it showed. "I don't care if he *was* due on the set an hour ago, Mr. LeRoy. Mr. Ebsen is a sick man." She slammed down the receiver.

Sick as I was, I remember laughing when I envisioned a frustrated Mervyn, furiously ejecting his chewed-up cigar and grabbing a new one from the elephant's foot.

It took two weeks of hospitalization and six weeks of recuperation to get me feeling like myself again. My vital signs were steady, except on one occasion. Nurses puzzled over my erratic chart figures the day after Halloween night and asked if I had experienced discomfort then. I remembered that I had been listening to the radio broadcast of Orson Welles's "War of the Worlds."

During treatment, my doctor, Charles Sturgeon, confronted the makeup man, Jack Dawn, for an analysis of the metallic powder used in my makeup as the Tin Man.

"Aluminum dust," Jack said. Then in righteous self-justification, he added, "*Pure* aluminum." It was like saying pure arsenic is better for you than the adulterated stuff. That was the problem. I had ingested pure aluminum; it had coated my lungs like paint.

A complication of my recovery was a symptom I had never experienced before or since. I felt as though my bloodstream was fermenting. It was nervous exhaustion, the doctor said. A nervous breakdown.

Really? A nervous breakdown? I had always sneered at the term, but no more. I learned there is in all of us a cushion of nervous accommodation which enables us to abide irritation and unpleasantness, but it is not inexhaustible. When it's depleted, watch out.

I reported back to the studio for work weeks later. Naturally I had been replaced. I had the feeling they regarded my bizarre illness with disbelief. They thought I was malingering because I didn't like the part. So they punished me by slamming me into a series of "B" pictures.

Meanwhile, back in *Oz*, the shooting went on. There was a new director, Victor Fleming, and a new actor, Jack Haley, in my part. For Jack's makeup, a silver paste was applied—no powder. All of the footage we had shot under Richard Thorpe had been scrapped.

Other accidents and unforeseen problems arose with the production as time went on. Margaret Hamilton, who played the Wicked Witch, was burned terribly on her face and hands when fiery special effects in her scene in Munchkinland went awry. The studio expected her to report back to work the next day.

After *The Wizard of Oz* was released—to lukewarm greetings considering its ultimate acclaim—I worked out my contract and left Metro in 1939. My next job was starring on Broadway that year in the musical comedy *Yokel Boy*. The show was not a smash, but it was a tremendous learning experience for me.

One long scene with actress Lois January was so badly written and ineptly played that nervous coughs from the audience almost drowned out what was being said on-stage. One night I counted the coughs. Twenty-seven. They were a nightly challenge, and I was determined to cut them down. And I did—to six—just by acting better.

I learned that the secret is simply, "make believe." You must make believe so well that you make the audience believe. It's as simple as that. And the lesson was to serve me well through several future television series. I was grow-ing; my talent was growing. I felt good about myself. I felt I was where I should be.

One night after the performance two visitors came backstage to see me. One was the MGM resident vocal coach and music coordinator, Roger Edens. The other was Judy Garland. I was flattered. Judy's career had soared since I last saw her, and she was now an important piece of MGM stu-dio property.

We chatted, exchanged compliments, laughed and groaned a little at the *Oz* reminiscences, and then Judy sur-prised me with a line. Gazing about her and with a gesture that indicated my new world, the world of theater, she said wistfully, "Someday I hope I can do something like this." I was astounded. Here was this attractive and talented teen-ager on the threshold of Hollywood superstardom, express-ing envy for my precarious little world of scratch and scram-ble: sudden closings, the gamble of it all, and the overall uncertainty of Broadway show business.

But I should not have been astounded. I should have known. She was feeling what I had felt when I said to the most powerful man in the motion picture business: "Here's the kind of fool I am, Mr. Mayer. You can't own me. I can't be a piece of goods on your counter." Judy's simple statement reflected the beginnings of her frustrations and foreshadowed the tragic events that finally destroyed her.

I sometimes wonder if there was some kind of a curse attached to the making of *The Wizard of Oz*. Along with Judy, most of the key participants have long since flown over the Great Rainbow. Perhaps I was lucky. The only scars I carry are a tendency toward bronchitis, with an occasional mysterious bronchial cough, and a need for air filtration systems in my home.

I also wonder if they really did scrap all the long shots from the ten days I was in the picture. I know my voice remains in the "We're Off to See the Wizard" musical number with the foursome locked arm in arm, skipping down that eternal Yellow Brick Road. Listen closely next time.

Also, I have a hunch that some economy-minded production man said to the cutter, "Hell, at this distance, you can't tell who is in the suit. Use what you've got."

WAR AND A PIECE

On Sunday, December 7, 1941, I was racing my Star-class boat in Santa Monica Bay. It was a momentous day for me. The race was the first I had ever won. Sailing on a euphoric cloud, I brought the *Moira* alongside the shore boat-landing float moored to Santa Monica Pier, so that David E. Baird (my crew) could get the trailer. Before I shoved off for the crane I overheard the Coast Guard auxiliary officer yell down to the shore boatman from topside: "Don't take any more Japs out to the fishing boats."

I wondered what the hell that meant. "Why not?" I asked the shore boatman. "What happened?"

"The Japs just bombed Pearl Harbor," he said.

My mind spun with the incredible meaning of the words. My instant reaction was, "Those crazy bastards . . .

they can't win." I was right, but it was to take four bloody years as well as the sacrifice of thousands of young lives and billions in treasure to prove it.

At 10:00 A.M. the next morning, David and I were down at the United States Naval Armory in Chavez Ravine, the scene of much heaving-about by hastily rallied reservists. It was a picture of agitated confusion: civilians milling about everywhere trying to enlist. David and I felt cool and superior. We had an appointment with a Commander Rimpau, arranged through my friend Commander Harvey Haislip, and we had a plan.

The reason the shore boatman got his orders to take no more Japanese out to their fishing boats was that one well-known local Japanese fisherman—whose sons were all named for American Presidents—was discovered to have fitted his boat with reserve diesel tanks of sufficient capacity to refuel a submarine. There were rumors of sub sightings just offshore and mysterious nocturnal lights from Palos Verdes, a coastal Japanese farming area.

From David's friend Dick Conklin we obtained carte blanche use of a sixty-five-foot schooner, *The Privateer*. Since we had heard the Navy was presently shy of offshore patrol vessels, why not load this yacht and others like it with communications equipment, along with .50-caliber machine guns and even depth charge racks to maintain an offshore submarine patrol? I learned much later that laying a depth charge pattern requires a minimum speed of fifteen knots. With the auxiliary engine speed capability of just six knots, dropping a depth charge from *The Privateer* (even at maximum depth setting) would only have succeeded in blowing us out of the water.

Commander Rimpau studied this naive, eager actor with quiet amusement. He assured me the Navy was handling the problem. Yeah, sure, I silently seethed, with the *Arizona* still burning. The Commander's attention shifted to my rugged Scottish crew friend, David Baird. When David recited his background and skills, Rimpau's eyes began to glitter. "Royal Canadian Air Force, World War I, participation in the *Zeebrüge* raid, seagoing in the North Sea fishing smacks and square-riggers on all seas and oceans, presently ship chandler," and most important, "a licensed, practicing electrical contractor." Before David was finished talking, Rimpau offered him, on behalf of the Navy, a Warrant Electrician rating—effective immediately. Warrant is the rate between chief and ensign. The recipient is a commissioned officer but only in a negative way. He *is* a commissioned officer, only he *isn't*.

Dave thought about three seconds, then shook his head no. "I was a noncom in the first one," he said. "If I go into any more wars, I'll go as a commissioned officer." And that was the end of that.

In time, the Navy established exactly the type of off-shore yacht patrol we had pitched that morning, but we were out of phase. By then, destiny had pointed my footsteps in another direction.

I was sitting in the bar at our residence in Pacific Palisades one morning working on a play when the phone rang. "Buddy," the voice said, "I want you to come right to my office. Have I got a script here for you—it's solid gold."

"Who is this?" I asked.

"Al Rosen. Drop everything and rush on down here. I guarantee this script will make you a million dollars, and you can put it on with spit."

"You mean it's a play?"

"It's the funniest farce ever written," Rosen said. "What a part for you. It will make you the hottest actor in the business. Now, I want you to come down to my office. . . ."

It was seventeen miles to his office, so I asked him to explain the part a little.

"You're this girl-shy professor, see?" Al said. "And your brother-in-law takes you to a stag party to get you over being shy. The party is raided, you escape over roofs and into a ladies' Turkish bath. The two of you put on sheets and ladies' wigs, and when a stripteaser comes in to take a bath and massage, you dive into the steam cabinet. Then—while you watch—the more she takes off, the more steam comes out of the cabinet."

I started to smile. "Al," I said, "I'll be right down."

The show was *Good Night, Ladies*. It cost, excluding a $3,000 equity bond, $6,000 to raise the curtain. It grossed between three and four million dollars and still holds Chicago records for money taken in by a stage show.

It all came about when dean of American dramatic critics George Jean Nathan commented in an article, "Where are the farces? Here we are in another war and there are no escapist theater farces. Where are the Avery Hopwood farces?" Between 1909 and the mid-20s Avery Hopwood wrote or coauthored a string of Broadway hits, among them: *Clothes*, *Seven Days*, *The Gold Diggers*, and *Ladies' Night in a Turkish Bath*, the original version of the show I was presently being pitched.

Little Al Rosen, who differed in the business from Big Al Rosen, the former manager of Loew's State in New York,

was a naughty little pixie of a man with a pornographic twinkle in his eye. He picked up cues quickly, as with Nathan's reference to farces, but when left to his own devices, tended to come up with shows having titles like *Mary Had a Little*.

When I read *Good Night, Ladies*, I knew it was basically funny and didn't need all the double-entendre lines in it. I insisted on the right to comb them out, which I did; this may have contributed to its success.

First produced in New York in 1917 as *Ladies' Night in a Turkish Bath* by Al Woods, this Hopwood farce was a bonanza. Our version was rewritten by Cyrus Wood, directed by Ed Clark Lilley and produced by Al Rosen and his partner Howard Lang. Besides myself, the cast consisted of two other males: Skeets Gallagher, a talented, skilled and lovable man, and Max Hoffman, Jr., born to and for the theater, the son of Gertrude Hoffman, the renowned variety *danseuse*. The rest of the cast were women: the loveliest, shapeliest, most talented actresses available in Hollywood at the time. They were carefully selected with an eye to balance so that those who were shy of talent or stage experience made up for it in looks, and vice versa. Although I didn't know it at the time, one of those girls was destined to change the course of my life.

We rehearsed three weeks and threw this concoction onto a stage at the Lobera Theatre in Santa Barbara shortly after a Japanese submarine was reported to have shelled the coast nearby. It's hard to say which was the greater shock—the Japanese attack or ours.

The Lobera was at that time a 99 percent cultural platform featuring string quartets, slide lectures and chamber music. I don't know what kind of a story Al Rosen gave to get us in, but afterward the Lobera was never quite the same. For one thing, as of the following Monday morning, there was a new "Admittance Committee." One reviewer who said the show stank, added the comment: "The *entr'acte* dialogue sparkled." Next day, Al Rosen waved a copy of the newspaper, indignantly proclaiming, "See, the guy contradicts himself. He says the show stinks—but the dialogue sparkles." Rosen didn't know that *entr'acte* means what the audience members say to each other during intermission.

The two performances in Santa Barbara served us well. They illustrated our problems and values. The comedy situations were sound. The cast was solid. We just needed playing time and a finish, so we headed for the Curran Theatre in San Francisco for two weeks to beat out the lumps. I learned two things about farce. First, you must—at all times—stay two seconds ahead of the audience; and second, the love story is as important as the jokes.

If you begin by enlisting the audience's concern over whether a man and woman finally overcome the obstacles to their uniting, then you must respect that concern and resolve it satisfactorily, no matter how wild the comedy becomes. Otherwise, the audience will go away feeling vaguely cheated.

Here's the *big* secret: People are basically "corny," no matter how sophisticated they think they are or appear to be, or how progressive or liberated they may seem. They want to see the boy and the girl get together. It's a little bouquet God built into the human propagation apparatus. When we recognized this, we found a finish for *Good Night, Ladies*—and we succeeded.

There is a game called "fruit basket upset," which couples used to play at parties. The women sat in chairs arranged in a circle. The men stood behind the chairs. One couple in the center had no chairs. The command, "Fruit basket upset!" was the signal for a wild melee where everyone changed chairs and partners and tried not to be singled out in the center and left with no chair. It was a great icebreaker. It stirred things up. Everybody wound up with a new partner.

That's the game the country was playing early in February of 1942. Some blamed it on the war, with its shattering of social mores and the acceptance of new behavior patterns. Families were dislocated. Husbands were constantly moving. Wives were left alone and became restless. There were brief encounters, which were attempts at escape from boredom or irritation. But great excitement. New faces. Forty-eight hour passes. We're shipping out in the morning, so live for tonight. A shucking off of old straitjackets; a feeling of being suddenly alive, even of growth, but above all—what the hell? Everybody else was doing it.

My nine-year marriage had stopped working some time before. It ended for a lot of the usual reasons, but emotional changes can develop over a long time, and sometimes you don't notice them while love slips away.

Once I was sitting on the curb in front of our house at 4:00 A.M., having just said goodbye to the last of our drinking, badminton-playing guests. My wife Ruth turned to me, and with more vehemence than I had ever heard her use she said into my face, "You're dull!"

Compared to what? I wondered. Why, compared, of course, to the last of the departing guests who happened to be an attractive male. "You're drinking too much," I said, while making a mental note that I must do something about my dullness. And now, thanks to Al Rosen's fateful phone call and the subtle scheme of destiny, I was in this show, in a "jumping" San Francisco, and the town was full of opportunities.

Call her Lola. She was a beautiful and splendid

WITH SKEETS GALLAGHER AT THE CHICAGO BLACKSTONE THEATRE IN 1942'S *GOOD NIGHT LADIES*. SKEETS'S BELLY LAUGH LINE: "IF THAT'S MY WIFE, I'LL BUY THAT DOOR!"

actress; her role in the show, a seductress.

"Ships are *SHEs*," I told her when we had dinner at Julius Castle and looked down on the remnant of the Pacific fleet that the Navy was hiding there below us. She listened like a little girl, while I pointed out the types of vessels: battleship, cruiser, transport, destroyer.

"Destroyer!" She pounced on the word joyously. "Which one is the destroyer?"

I pointed it out again and she admired its sleek lines and then laughed her husky, throaty laugh. Her eyes sparkled as she embraced her role in society. "That's what I am," she said, her eyes now full of smoldering fire. "A destroyer."

"You're such a sweet and clean and good little fellow," she told me later. "Somebody ought to dirty you up a little."

So she did.

And for anyone who feels called upon to judge and assign the guilt or innocence or invaded moralities of the events that followed, I could never plead that I was put upon. I never called the police.

While we were in San Francisco perfecting the show, our senior producer Howard Lang sent Al Rosen to Chicago to find us a theater. It was not an easy job, due to the local prejudices; it was thought that all productions originating on the West Coast were trash. Nevertheless, Al sent back glowing reports. After being snubbed by the Shuberts (controllers of the most desirable theaters, the Selwyn and the Harris), he had found the vacant Blackstone, which was a white elephant due to gas rationing and the fact that it was some distance out from "The Loop."

He had made a good deal. It was a 70-30 split after the break-even point. Al also had achieved a promotional plum—a scheduled welcome of the company by Mayor Kelly on the steps of City Hall.

When we arrived, however, a glance at the story running in the middle of the front page of the *Chicago Tribune* hinted that the meeting with the mayor probably would not occur. The caption read: "Hollywood Producer Held On Rape Charge."

Al's story held up: While he was showering, a prostitute guest filched the contents of his wallet. He called the police, and the girl countered with a phony rape charge.

Contrary to our apprehensions, Al's misadventure had no adverse effect on our opening. If anything, the event enhanced it.

The critics welcomed us with "money" reviews, such as, "It ain't art, just dressed up burlesque—but I wish I had a piece of it."

I had a piece. A big piece. My salary, plus a vested interest of $16\frac{2}{3}$ percent and, of course, my romantic interest—Lola.

Chicago stampeded to our box office.

Overnight, the show became the hottest ticket in town, and the Shuberts were furious because we weren't in one of their theaters. In addition to captivating all segments of the populace (socialites, truck drivers, soldiers, sailors,

Catholic priests), we did repeat business. One group bought the front row every Saturday night during the entire run.

Despite this period of personal economic bonanza, the fact that the war was going against us in the South Pacific bugged my conscience; this was especially so while performing for an audience half composed of service people in uniform while I cavorted about the stage rigged as a female.

Further discomfort and complications were provided by my wife, Ruth, who suddenly arrived in town. She had decided I wasn't so dull after all and maybe worth competing for.

One night Ruth approached the actress she suspected of wrecking our home, just before Lola's entrance on stage, and told her, "Stay away from my husband, or I'll cut your goddamn throat!" From that point on, the war seemed to me a far more peaceful place to be.

Jim Keefe, our PR man, forwarded to Skeets and me a request from Commander Goldenson, who was in charge of local Navy recruiting. We were to come to the processing center and just chat with the stream of young men waiting in the slow induction line.

While I was there, I made another run at the Navy; I asked Commander Goldenson what kind of rating I might get if I enlisted. With my two years of college education, he said, I would be a sucker not to shoot for a commission, provided I knew celestial navigation and had some experience with twin-engine boats.

Feeling confident I could be replaced in the show, I promptly enrolled in the Great Lakes Cruising Club navigation course, and in record time completed it *cum laude*.

Andy Berky was a friend who owned my favorite dining place, The Key Club, on the near North Side: he also had a forty-foot twin-engine cruiser, the *Behave Yourself*, which he had volunteered to the Navy League for use in letting the Great Lakes Naval Training Station's Abbott Hall naval officer trainees—the "Ninety Day Wonders"—actually get experience afloat.

Somehow, I persuaded him to put me in charge of the boat, so early every morning I would pick up a load of aspiring "future admirals" at the Navy Pier and take them out on Lake Michigan. I taught them what I knew about seamanship and boat handling.

In one respect it was the blind leading the blind because I was simultaneously learning how to maneuver this twin-engine beauty. Fortunately, with my previous sailing experience, plus a natural feel for a vessel afloat, it was no great chore.

Despite my positive background, my meticulous preparations, and my sincere ambition to become an officer in the United States Navy, my commission never arrived. What did arrive was a curt form letter stating that my application had been rejected. A knowledgeable friend theorized that it was because my father had been born too close to Germany.

This second rejection by the Navy was a shattering blow. But after a few days of quiet rage, I rationalized: To hell with them. My destiny lay elsewhere. I will stay out of the damned war, make a lot of money, and have a lot of fun.

At the stage door one night, casually saluting the girls, there stood a handsome naval lieutenant in a long dark-blue bridge coat, blue-baker cap, lieutenant's shoulder boards, and a white scarf. After a beat of puzzlement, the girls screamed in delight when they recognized Walter Kane.

Kane, a Hollywood actor's agent, was probably the last person I would have expected to see in this garb. I was consumed with envy.

"Walter, you son of a bitch," I said. "Where the hell did you get that costume?"

"You want one?" he taunted. "Come over next door to the Balinese Room and meet my boss."

That's how I met Jim Kimberly. Jim was a Lieutenant Commander in the United States Coast Guard Reserve, a charming man who literally glittered with gold; he had gold buttons and braid on his uniform, tinted gold-rimmed glasses, a massive nugget shaped into a signet ring on his finger,

and a heavy gold ID bracelet on his wrist. As the son of a founder of Kimberly-Clark paper goods company, one could safely assume Jim's pockets were also lined with the glittery stuff. The thought occurred to me that if he ever fell overboard he'd sink like a stone. Jim, an avid yachtsman, and I hit it off right from the start in a friendship that was to endure and grow over fifty years.

From the Balinese Room of the Blackstone, we took off on a tour of the town, powered by boilermakers along the way. During the evening, I must have signed something because three weeks later there arrived from Washington a cylindrical mailer, which, when opened, disgorged a document signed by the President of the United States.

It read: "By Order of the President, you, Christian Ebsen, are now an officer and a gentleman in the United States Coast Guard with the rank of Lieutenant Junior Grade."

Jim called later to apologize for the delay. His boss, Admiral Donohue, needed some convincing that this nut, who actually wanted to trade his successful show job for sea duty, was not a deranged Section Eight case.

When the full impact of this major happening materialized, my spirit soared.

That I could so readily turn my back on the land and transfer my devotion to a ship, I attribute to the blood of my Viking ancestors.

At my first step on deck, I felt an inner calm which told me I was where I should be. Sleeping aboard that first night, I actually pitied the people who had to sleep ashore. That was while the ship was tied to the dock. The sea was later to test and temper this passion.

USS *POCATELLO* ON WHICH I SERVED AS 1ST LIEUTENANT
AND LATER, EXECUTIVE OFFICER FROM 1943 TO 1945.
I AM THIRD FROM THE RIGHT ON THE FOREDECK.

My transition from actor to naval officer began with four months of general indoctrination and two months of specialization in antisubmarine warfare at St. Augustine, Florida.

Although the Coast Guard, in some Navy circles, is sneered at as the "shallow water" or "hooligan Navy," the fact is, in wartime it becomes an integral part of the Navy. Furthermore, Coast Guard personnel attending Navy specialization schools, spurred by pride, characteristically populated the top ten positions in their class—so I had a position from which to sneer back.

In spite of roadblocks, I had made it! Through the backdoor, perhaps, but I *was* in the Navy.

We shook down in the waters off San Diego after our ship, the patrol frigate USS *Pocatello*, was commissioned at Kaiser Yard #4 in Richmond, California.

The testing of our proficiency in the job we were trained for, antisubmarine warfare, was presided over by Cal Tech "hotshots," who came aboard with their clipboards and observed, while we simulated attacks on a "tame" submerged submarine.

When they told us our score was second only to the Navy destroyer escort *England*, which had a "kill" record in the South Pacific of six Japanese subs in seven days, our spirits went through the overhead. We were a Gung Ho Ship! Ready to take on the whole Japanese Navy!

Then one day our Skipper, Sammy Guill, summoned his eight officers to the wardroom for an announcement.

"Gentlemen," he said, "I assure you this is for one patrol only, but we have just been designated a weather ship."

From our previous "high," our spirits now went through the deck.

It meant the Navy had assigned us to Station "Able," a two-hundred-mile circle of Pacific Ocean sixteen hundred miles due west of Seattle, where we would bounce around for a month at a time, sending up weather balloons and gathering the data to be fed to the Navy's navigational information network. Important stuff, of course, but why us? A unit so perfectly honed to sink enemy subs? Why? Because there were no Japanese subs operating in the North Pacific, and, very simply, somebody had to do it.

In spite of the Captain's promise, "one patrol only," a year later we were *still* doing it.

By then I clearly understood the character of the future Mister Roberts. I was living his role on the *Pocatello*.

But frustration and low morale were becoming evident

AS MR. ROBERTS IN THE STAGE PLAY OF *MR. ROBERTS*. 1947

aboard, emerging among the crew in the form of perforated ulcers, suicide attempts, and letters home containing fantastic accounts of nonexistent battles we had won. We officers were required to censor those letters.

It verified the truth of something I had once read about war: It's 10 percent action and 90 percent boredom. Our share wasn't even 10 percent. It was a frustrating discovery for me to realize that in my zeal to be a warrior for my country, I had blindly turned my back on my primary talent: the ability to entertain, to lighten spirits, and to make life more endurable.

What our ship needed most right then was entertainment, and that's what I turned to. Using the talent aboard, I wrote, cast and directed small shows, which had a strong entertainment value. And they were rehearsed and performed under astonishing circumstances.

The rehearsals often produced more laughs for the crew than the performances. It gave everyone something to think about, discuss and overcome. One production I did of *H.M.S. Pinafore* was interrupted in mid-performance by a radar contact, so the cast had to rush to General Quarters in their show costumes. This resulted in such remarkable sights as British Jack Tars manning twenty-millimeter guns, and Sir Joseph Porter, K.C.B, Admiral of the Queen's Navy, as third loader on a three-inch fifty.

As the tide of war began to turn in our favor, we began to see far down the tunnel the glimmerings of hope that promised ultimate victory. My former frustrations at being barred from the service turned into apprehension that the war would be over, and I could never claim to have done anything in it but send up weather balloons and study the flight characteristics of gooney birds.

My motivation was now completely turned around. This wasn't why I had joined. Now I wanted to get out—at least to *see* some of the war. A plan began to form in my mind.

During a thirty-day leave, I flew to New York and talked to three people: Abe Lastfogel, Larry Phillips and Elliot Nugent. Lastfogel and Phillips headed the USO, and Elliot had written the comedy *Male Animal*, which I had played in summer stock. The plan was for Elliot and me to assemble and rehearse a company of the play and for the USO to send it out through the European Theater as troop entertainment. In this way I would feel I was actually contributing my best talent to the war effort. Having received the green light from Lastfogel, Phillips and Nugent, I flew to Washington to request orders from the Coast Guard that would allow me to pursue this mission. Admiral Donahue acquiesced. There was one more hurdle: Navy Personnel.

The admiral in Navy Personnel slowly read my orders, then looked up and made a momentous pronouncement. "You are a qualified seagoing naval officer," he told me.

I stood straight and tall, thrilled by the words. It was the sort of a verbal diploma I had striven for originally. "Yes sir," I said. He then made a short notation, handed me back the papers and said, "Request denied. The Navy cannot spare you."

Oh, mountain-peak of irony! The Navy that didn't want any part of me (*twice!*), now could not do without me.

Back on the *Pocatello* the situation was normal, only more so. The men were "goldbricking," shirking their duties. Officers, who had gone sloppy, were not even reprimanding them. The Captain had been transferred. The

Gunnery Officer, "Honest John" Wynn, was now in command. I found I had inherited the job of "Exec." Morale was a shambles. No one wanted to be aboard anymore. It was a ship without spirit, without heart.

One night as I stood the 1200 to 0400 watch, the wind was piping up ten knots above the normal forty-five and changing direction. Suddenly it came on the beam, causing a confused sea, with waves crashing into the ship out of the night from all directions. This continuous irregular impact of tons of water hitting us midships created a jerking lurch and a torturous wracking strain on the hull. Through my feet on the deck I was getting a message that wasn't good. It aroused the specter of chronic, often-repaired weld-tears. I wondered if the damned ship was coming apart.

These sucker punches of the sea produce an overwhelming physical fatigue as the body is asked to accommodate more than the normal lift and fall of the ship's motion. The fatigue generated a feverish irritation with everything around me. When relieved of my watch, it was in this mood that I arrived in the wardroom, having cautiously clawed and crawled my way down from the bridge in the dark.

The typical wardroom coffee, an overcooked brew that resembles molasses, suggested to me that I switch to milk, which I removed from the refrigerator. Setting the gallon glass jar on the sideboard, I poured myself a glass, made a cheese sandwich and prepared to relax while reading the morning news flashes thumbtacked to the bulletin board. I had reached for the milk to stow it when our craft collided with the granddaddy of all waves, a tremendous broadside impact that heeled the ship over forty-five degrees. The milk hit the deck with a splintering crash, along with my sand-

wich, various kitchen utensils and me. Fortunately I was able to avoid landing on the deadly shards of the milk container and only wound up with the handle of the orange squeezer about to become *alarmingly* intimate.

There aren't enough expletives to fully express my exact feelings at such a time. Besides, when destiny deals me a hand which is simply unplayable, I tend to laugh—or to *write* something about it.

In this instance I was inspired to write a song. The song, like most of today's movies, has words in it regarded as obscene; but in order to write the truth about men serving on a ship at sea in time of war, those words are indispensable to convey the true mood and feelings of the world in which the crew and I had come to live. The theme of the song was the profound and classic ambivalence of the eternal Mariner toward his possessive environment—"The (with a slight interpolation) *Loving* Sea."

Upon request of the crew, I resumed my established practice of staging concerts. At the next one, I sang my song. Their reaction was predictable—positive and raucous.

But it was therapeutic! Surprisingly—beyond its brazen vulgarities the song seemed to have a profound meaning to them. One man came up to me later. "Gee, Mister Ebsen," he said, with misty eye and a deep sincerity bordering on awe, "we didn't know you officers felt the same way about it as we did."

Eureka! I had communicated!

One enterprising yeoman asked for a copy of the words, which I gave him. He then mimeographed the sheet and sold copies to the crew for 10¢ each. And it went into extra printings! My first song hit!

Morale on the ship seemed to improve after that. Had my song made a contribution to "understanding"? Could this song have been my most telling contribution to the war effort? Who knows?

At any rate, we dutifully completed our assigned mission and learned to count our blessings, usually after reading the casualty lists. After all, who in their right mind wants to be shot at? Some sobering news advised us that the DE *England*, which had sunk the six subs in seven days, was herself sunk shortly afterward.

But fortunes vary.

Walter Kane, who "agented" me into this job, came out of the war a minor hero, having served as a beach master in Marine landings in the South Pacific.

Some days—deep in my heart—I still envy him.

PACKING THEM IN WHILE BRINGING BACK VAUDEVILLE. 1947

Chapter 11

NOBODY COUNTS YOU OUT BUT YOURSELF

My first job, after accumulating the points to get out of the service, was again obtained through the fortuitous cooperation of Howard Reinheimer and Oscar Hammerstein.

The production was Oscar's 1946 revival of *Showboat*.

It was an easy job at a good salary and afforded me the time to demilitarize my mind and retool it to compete once again in civilian life.

But when *Showboat* closed in January 1947, after a year's run at the Ziegfeld Theatre in New York, it marked the beginning of a seven-year economic plague for me, during which I didn't gross as much as a box boy. Having been divorced and remarried while in the service, I had an added responsibility: alimony.

A week before *Showboat* closed, Abe Lastfogel came by

WITH COLETTE LYONS IN THE 1946 REVIVAL OF *SHOWBOAT*.

my table one night in Toots Shor's restaurant, where working actors went for after-work sustenance, plus a status-bestowing "insult" by Toots, the head "Crumbum" (that was his welcome—"Hello, Crumbum!").

"What are you going to do now that the show is closing?" Abe asked.

"Look for another job," I told him.

"Come by the office," he said. "Maybe we can help you."

The "Office" was the William Morris Agency, the most powerful theatrical agency in the world, and Abe had approached *me*. It was reassuring. The day I arranged to come by the office I ran into Garson Kanin in a corridor. Gar had written the play *Born Yesterday*, which was then the hottest ticket on Broadway. We chatted and I told him why I was there. He said, "Come on. I'll go in with you." A more providential and prestigious entrance could not have been arranged.

In the board room at the long mahogany table sat the heads of every department in the agency: theater, motion picture, nightclub, radio, summer stock, and the burgeoning television field. The ringmaster, smiling Abe Lastfogel, approached to greet us. Gar didn't wait. Stretching high to put his arm around me, he took charge.

"Listen, you sons of bitches," he said, "this is my boy. You take care of him or you'll hear from me. Ya' hear?"

Needless to say, the meeting was a tremendous success. Their feverish interest in my career sent me out on a cloud. I had signed with the William Morris office. I'm sure everyone in that room was sincere. I'm sure they all tried, but six months later the score was a mere three weeks in summer stock plus countless one-night stands in every picture theater in Brooklyn, the Bronx, Staten Island and the Shine circuit. It was a fruitless effort to bring back vaudeville. For the Shine dates I got $50 a night, minus a 10 percent commission and a 5 percent booking fee.

One manager took me aside as he paid me off. In great embarrassment he said, "The last time you played this theater you were up on the screen dancing. You were a star. Why are you doing this?"

"For the money," I said as I took it from his hand. It was the truth. I was glad to get the work, and I was grateful to John Lastfogel, a lower echelon nephew who worked his heart out to get me the dates. Joe Magee, who booked me in summer stock, was another unsung hero in the Morris office. But with all of their efforts and everyone's good intentions, my gross income at year's end was only $7,000. My salary in *Showboat* had been $750 a week, and my previous motion picture salary was $2,000 a week. I didn't need a graph to alert me that I was going downhill.

In December 1947, John Lastfogel booked me into a club in New London. It catered to sailors and had a normal security complement of two cops and three shore patrol. It was located in the low rent district, and the raffish foot traffic passing its sleazy storefront entrance in no way fulfilled the promise of elegance suggested by its name, The London Terrace. The customers were noisy and vocal and had a short attention span. They liked some of my dancing, especially the gag dance I did with my wirehaired terrier, Hobo. I gained some respect with an improvisation, tying fancy sailor knots. My engagement there can only be rated among my lesser triumphs.

I took a snapshot of the entrance to the place when I

left, and upon my return to New York I had my cabdriver take me to the Ziegfeld Theatre, where I also took a picture. With festive seasonal paper and a bottle of glue, I construct-ed a Christmas card for Abe Lastfogel.

"Dear Abe," I began. Next to a picture of the Ziegfeld in all of its art deco elegance, I wrote "From *here* . . . " and on the reverse side I pasted the snap of the London Terrace. (In the shot were two crummy-looking street people in confer-ence. They looked like dope pushers concluding a deal.) Under the second picture I wrote, ". . . to *here* in less than a year. Congratulations and Merry Christmas! Buddy Ebsen."

Abe was stung. He made a special effort to locate me, then called, filled with defensive embarrassment. He want-ed me to come in for another full-dress meeting with "the boys." I told him I'd think about it.

Meanwhile, my friend and lawyer Howard Reinheimer called because he was worried about me; he knew I had been struggling. We got together and had a long, serious discussion. He came up with an idea. He had a per-sonal relationship with William Morris, Jr., the titular head of the agency. Howard would set up a meeting for me with Bill. We could sit down and talk, and perhaps something good would stem from it.

Couldn't hurt, I agreed. Instantly the glimmerings of a plan began to unfold in my mind: In those days, Milton Berle was the unchallenged King of Television. He used acts that he could invade and end up being the funny one. What could be more natural than Miltie in drag—which he loved—doing some of the routines my sister Vilma and I used to do. Berle was with the William Morris Agency. It was perfect. A word from Howard's friend, Bill Morris, and

I'd be on the Berle show.

I charged into Morris's office beaming with confidence. There he was, behind a big polished desk. A picture of old-time entertainer Harry Lauder hung on the wall behind him, along with a shot of a Scottish regiment of kilted "Ladies from Hell" advancing with fixed bayonets under fire. There was also a picture of his father, William Morris, Sr., who had first booked Harry Lauder into the Palace.

Bill got up and affably shook hands with me. He sat down and prepared to listen to my story. As I launched into my brilliant scenario, I became aware that his manner was slowly changing. He was smiling less and suddenly not at all, but I pressed on. The flop-sweat began to ooze at my temples. After a beat he gave me one of the kindliest smiles I have ever received. It was compassionate and fatherly.

"Buddy," he said, "what I'm going to tell you, you may not like me for today, but in years to come you'll thank me. Why don't you retire from show business?"

There was silence. The blankness of my face fully advertised my incapability to speak. Had I swallowed a live hand grenade and had it exploded in my stomach, I couldn't have been more stunned.

"You used to be half of a cute brother 'n' sister dance team," he tried to explain. "But you're not anymore. And like a lot of other performers before you, there comes a time in life when you've got to face that."

I just sat there staring at him.

"Get out now while you can. Gracefully. Sell cars or insurance or something. Maybe real estate."

All I could say was, "What about the Berle show?"

He shook his head. "Not a chance."

I persisted. "Howard and I thought if you spoke to him—put in a word. . . ." He shook his head again. "It won't do any good."

"But Berle is a client of yours," I hung on. "You must have some influence. . . ." Then he gave it to me straight. "We tried. Berle doesn't want you." I could say nothing more. He looked at me with great compassion.

"It's over, kid. Get out now while you can—gracefully."

Finally, when I rose I thanked him for the interview and stumbled from the room. I was choking back tears. Tears of *rage*.

Time cut: Seventeen years later.

The scene: My "Beverly Hillbillies" dressing room bungalow at the General Service Studios, Hollywood.

Discovered: Hedda Hopper, the famous syndicated Hollywood columnist and me.

Practical props: Tacos and champagne.

During the seventeen-year interlude, the wheel of fortune had turned for me. I had done three television series, "Davy Crockett" and "Corky and the White Shadow" for Disney and "Northwest Passage" for MGM. I had established myself as a legitimate actor in films like *Breakfast at Tiffany's*. I had made numerous guest appearances on television shows like "The Ed Wynn Show," "The Danny Thomas Show" and "The Hollywood Palace." I had replaced Elliot Nugent in the Broadway production of *Male Animal* and was presently starring as Jed Clampett in a show that had been number one in the ratings for two consecutive years and was still going strong.

During that time I had encountered Milton Berle only once, at an Archie Moore fight. He leaped over three rows of seats to glad-hand Max Baer, Jr., and me. "Gee, you guys are number one," he enthused. Then with a nostalgic, faraway look in his eyes he added, "I was number one once." I actually felt sorry for him.

"Like some coffee, Hedda?"

Over Mexican coffee and a cigarette, Hedda voiced her usual demand.

"I need a story, kid. Come on," she said. "Give me a story."

I thought a moment, then started to grin.

"Well," she said.

"I've got a story—one that's never been told. But you can't use it," I told her.

"Why not?" she bullied.

"I don't want to embarrass anyone," I explained.

"What is it? Tell me. I won't use it."

"Scout's honor?" I asked.

She gave me the salute. "Scout's honor."

So I told her the story about William Morris, Jr., and me.

The next morning, it was the lead paragraph in her column in the *Los Angeles Times*.

Then the phone began to ring. First it was the William Morris office at various official levels with protestations, recriminations and denials. And finally, the main event. It was about 4:00 P.M. when Bill Morris, Jr., called from Malibu. He had retired there, having quit show business—"gracefully."

"Jesus, kid," he began somewhat hysterically. "How could you do this to me? I'm the guy who encouraged you. Don't you remember? When you and your sister came up from Florida, I'm the guy who. . . ." He went on at some length. He said he was thrilled with my comeback, but, "Jesus, kid—how could you?"

When he finally stopped talking, I said, "Bill, listen to me. I'm not mad. I'm grateful. You once said I'd thank you for the advice and I do. And please get it straight. This is no *comeback*. I'm farther ahead now than I ever was before, and I thank you for it. I thank you for making me mad enough to stay *in* show business."

HEDDA HOPPER, FAMOUS HOLLYWOOD COLUMNIST. 1962

Chapter 12

AUDREY

It was one of those jobs that just happened out of the blue. The phone rang. Blake Edwards told me he had a part. If I would test for it and get it, he wanted to bet me a case of champagne that I would get an Academy Award nomination. I tested for it and got the part, never really minding not getting the champagne because the experience is one of the most cherished of my career.

Playing a scene with Audrey Hepburn was like trying on an exquisitely tailored sports coat for the very first time. There was a free-flowing instinct about her that filled the cracks of my own deficiencies.

No two takes are identical. The "nowness" of one minute ago is gone forever and can only be played back—never duplicated. In one's delivery the timing varies by split

THE LOVELY AUDREY HEPBURN.

N CO-STARS WITH AUDREY HEPBURN IN BREAKFAST AT TIFFANY'S

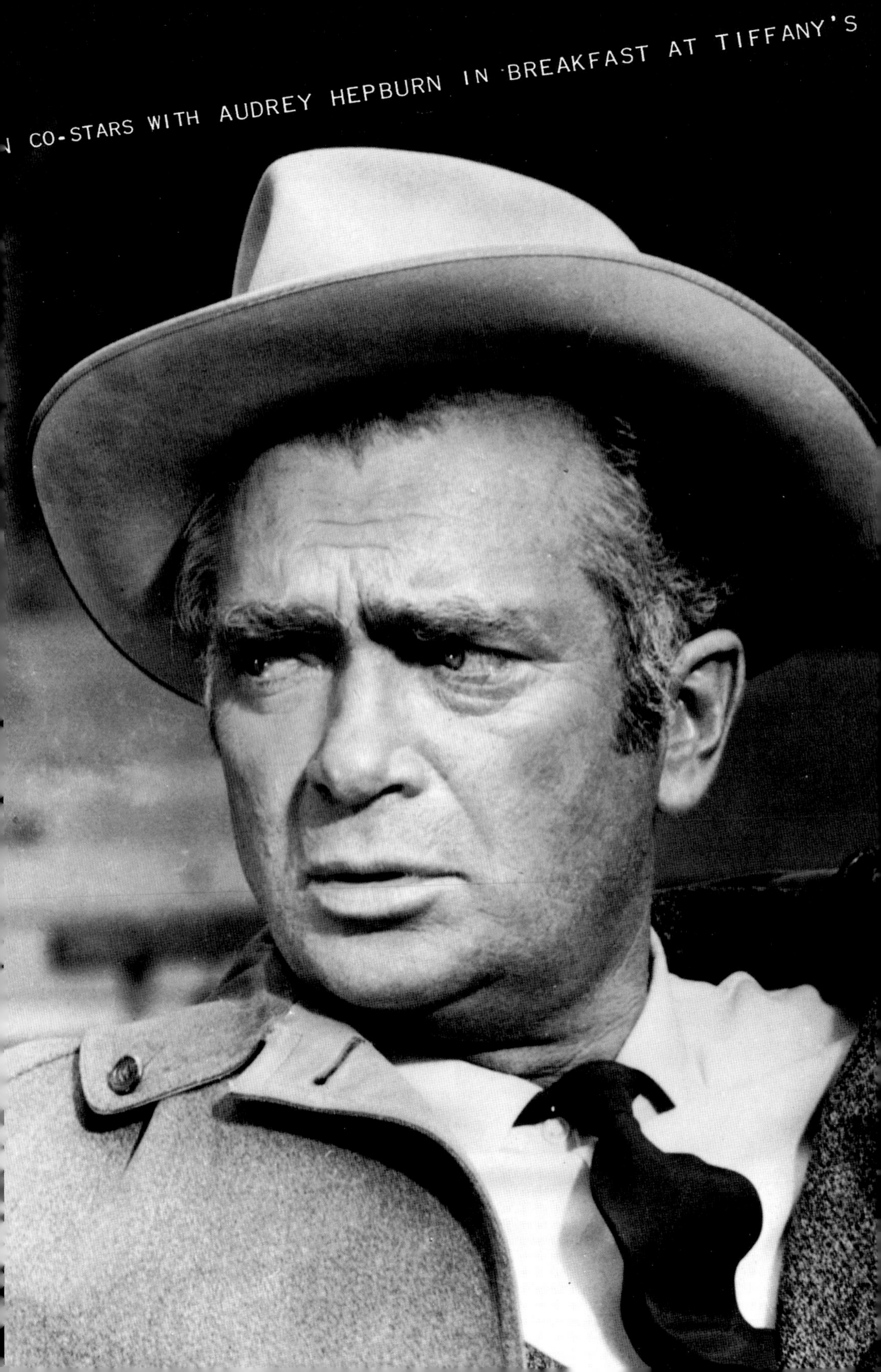

seconds, or the weight on a word switches by audible millidecibels.

However differently done on each take, Audrey's talent was such that it supplied the perfect counterpart instinctively, almost imperceptibly. When a scene was over, my artistic conscience immediately told me it was right: I had that good *feeling*. Such is my recollection of working with Audrey in *Breakfast at Tiffany's*, a 1961 film version of the Truman Capote story.

I saw Audrey Hepburn only once after the finish of the picture. It was at my bank in Beverly Hills. Dressed in faded blue jeans, a well-worn shirt, floppy sandals and large dark glasses, she needed to cash a check. She looked nothing like the glamorous superstar with whom I had just completed a motion picture. Because the teller was square and Audrey's check sizable, she was having problems.

It is among my warmest memories that I was privileged to *vouch* for Audrey Hepburn.

Anyway, about the Oscar—things were a little mixed up that year. That was the year George C. Scott spurned his nomination. Sometimes I think if they hadn't wasted one on him—maybe—? Oh, well, I have no gripes. Scenes with Audrey Hepburn made it all worthwhile.

TV GUIDE

Local Programs May 6-12
30¢

TV Sex
Raising Eyebrows—
And Ratings
Page

Buddy Ebsen
of "Barnaby Jones"

TELEVISION

In 1942, when Skeets Gallagher and I were starring in *Good Night, Ladies* at the Blackstone Theatre in Chicago, our press agent Jim Keefe came to us one day and described an interesting scientific experiment being conducted on one of the upper floors of a Balaban and Katz movie theater. It was a device that broadcast *over the airwaves* an image being enacted in front of a camera, and it could be viewed by "receiving sets" scattered among the general populace. This bizarre innovation was called, he said, "television." Jim suggested we might gain a little free publicity for the show by appearing on it. And so we did.

I took along my little wirehaired terrier, Hobo, and before we knew it, Skeeter, Hobo and I were in a primitive studio making our first appearance on this pioneering form

ILLUSTRATION ON THE COVER OF *TV GUIDE.*
MAY, 1978

of communication.

First, Skeets and I did a little improvised comedy patter. Then Hobo joined us and snapped a cookie from his nose on command, did a little dance with me, and for a finish jumped into my arms. (You might say that was television's first Stupid Pet Trick, popularized much later on "Late Night with David Letterman.") During our television performance, I observed a small illuminated box alongside the camera. The light coming from it was a greenish hue, and there were heavy black striations running horizontally across the screen. In its center were ghostly figures moving about—two tall and one small. I was told the box was called a monitor. And the ghostly images?

"That's you," the camera operator said. "That's what is going out on the air." I thought I wasn't hearing right.

"That's what's going out on the air?" I echoed.

"That's right."

"How many receiving sets are out there?" I asked.

"In the state? Thirty-seven," he told me. I was astounded. That grown men would spend time, energy and money on this obvious boondoggle! It was truly beyond belief. I was miffed at Jim for trapping us in this childish nonsense. Before we left the studio, I pontificated: "This will never amount to anything."

Today, fifty-one years and six television series later—two of which poured more dollars into my pocket than a thousand *Good Night, Ladies* performances—I am inclined to revise my opinion.

By 1945, when I emerged from my three years in the armed services, television production companies and televised programs were hatching all over the place. Some folded quickly, some survived for a time, and some evolved into the flourishing entities they are today.

Because I could sing, dance, act—and, most important, remember my lines—I got a good share of the guest appearances available. Another leg-up was that I did not freeze when that little red light went on. I did "The Ed Wynn Show," "Chevrolet TV Theatre," "Climax," "Playhouse 90," and I even presided as MC of the half-hour show commemorating the connection of the coaxial cable at Cleveland, a new device which enabled New York and Chicago producers to air their shows simultaneously, live in both markets.

Perhaps the most important show I ever performed in at that time was the televising of a John Steinbeck story, "The House." An independent producer named Eugene Solow bought three Steinbeck stories and produced a very short miniseries. Thomas Mitchell starred in one, Lew Ayres in another and I in the third. This was a validation of a lesson I had learned from Benny Davis: Always do your very best every time you're at bat. You never know who is going to be watching or what the job may lead to.

Walt Disney had been toying with the notion of doing a motion picture about Davy Crockett for eighteen years. He thought first of animating the story. When Walt realized that live actors work cheaper than cartoon characters, he turned the project over to Norman Foster with instructions to "find a Crockett."

Norman was an actor-turned-director. Some people found him flighty. Perhaps it was true, but he was much more. To me, he will always be a sensitive gentleman with a sense of humor and an impeccable artistic conscience. When he saw me in "The House," he called Disney and announced, "I've found your Davy Crockett." He borrowed a copy of the kinescope and showed it to Walt. Disney was half sold. Norman called me with the news, and I celebrated.

Then Walt happened to see a picture called *Them*, about giant ants. In it a young actor, playing a highway patrolman, is locked up as a suspected nut after describing his sightings of gigantic insects. It was only a two-minute scene, but when it was over Walt said, "That's Davy Crockett." The young actor's name was Fess Parker, and the rest is history.

WALT DISNEY. CIR. 1950

Walt Disney's approach to television was very ingenious. He reversed the established order of making a film, showing it first in theaters, then on television. "Davy Crockett, King of the Wild Frontier," and "Davy Crockett and the River Pirates" premiered on television. Later, segments of the show "King of the Wild Frontier," cut together as a feature film, grossed enough to make Disney very happy with his decision. In view of the commotion it created at the time, "Crockett" is perceived today by the general public as a long-run success made up of many episodes. Actually, there were only five, which were shown repeatedly by popular demand.

Norman Foster was apologetic when he called to tell me I was not to be Crockett. I was crushed, of course, but then he called to tell me about the role of Georgie Russel.

The filming of the "Crockett" episodes were some of the most rugged location expeditions I have ever experienced. (The Disney production people had dealt primarily with animated filming and were naive about what constituted a well-organized location operation.)

First of all, there were stunts involved. But they had sent along only one stunt man. Now Fess is 6' 5" and I am 6' 3½" The stunt man was 5'-by-5'. So Fess and I wound up doing our own stunts. In the course of filming, I figure I qualified for four Purple Hearts.

The most dangerous incident involved a muzzle-loading musket, which blew up in my face. In the explosion and flash, I lost my eyelashes, my eyebrows, and a good patch of my front hairline. It was a scary threat to my eyesight as well, so the crew rushed me to a hospital to have my eyes irrigated. Obviously the incident shook up the front office on the coast because they wanted hourly reports on my condition.

The other incidents were less painful and less serious. In one, Fess and I did a fast ride, and in the dismount from our horses, Fess's foot contacted the stock of my long rifle. It pivoted in my hand, so the barrel came up and struck my temple a sharp blow, knocking me cold.

Later on in the filming, Fess and I were leading a squadron of mounted soldiers across a shallow lake. No one had bothered to check the bottom of the lake. It turned out to be bottomless, quicksand-like mud, so when our horses started sinking into it, they panicked. Those of us who didn't get thrown, quickly dismounted, but we still got trampled and cut up as we tried to lead our frantic animals through the sucking mud, which was seeded with broken

"DAVY CROCKETT AND THE RIVER PIRATES." 1954

bottles and old tin cans.

Another misfortune was actually kind of funny. In the story, Georgie Russel was to approach Crockett with a precious letter from Davy's wife. Foster had set up the camera so that my path intercepted a circle of townsfolk doing a country dance. The plan was to have me trapped in the dance, then to be shoved into the center to "shine" and do my big step—the Bandy Twist. Then I was to retreat into the circle of townsfolk who were moving clockwise in a path that would take me past the camera in a close-up. Here, I would step out of the circle, approach Fess, hand him the letter and say, "Here's a letter for you, Davy."

It was a splendidly innovative shot requiring perfect timing and extensive rehearsal, largely because of the inexperienced locals playing the townspeople. We went through

FESS PARKER PORTRAYS DAVY CROCKETT, AND I PLAY HIS LIFELONG FRIEND
GEORGIE RUSSEL IN "DAVY CROCKETT AND THE RIVER PIRATES." 1954

it many times, and something always went wrong. Norman Foster's patience was running low. In fact, he was at the screaming stage. We tried the shot once more, and I knew this had to be it.

On the next take, everything was working beautifully. Timing was perfect. When I was shoved into the center to do my Bandy Twist, I did it with just a little extra abandon. Too much. As I twisted and spun, my powder horn, connected to a leather thong, took off and began twirling around my neck. It started orbiting my head rapidly, winding closer and closer, wrapping around my neck with increasing velocity. When it struck my head just over my left eye, I almost went down for the count, but through my grogginess I knew I had to continue and carry on for Norman. So I staggered back into the circle, dancing toward the camera. Halfway there I felt something warm and sticky trickling down my face. When I arrived for the close-up, I stepped out of the circle, handed Fess the letter and said, "Here's a letter for you, Davy."

"Cut! Beautiful!" Norman yelled. His reaction snap-shifted from ecstasy to angry recrimination when I turned my head, and he saw the blood running down my face. "Oh goddamnit, you're bleeding!"

"I tried not to, Norman," I apologized.

There was a two-inch gash over my left eyebrow, bleeding profusely. We had no doctor on the set, and our medical needs were served by a young ex-Navy pharmacist's mate who carried some Band-Aids, Mercurochrome and insect repellent in a small, black satchel. The hospital was eleven miles away. Company manager Henry Spitz pleaded with me. Would I allow the pharmacist's mate to try to stop the blood-flow with collodion so everyone could

finish the day's work? Then later I'd be rushed to the hospital to be properly stitched up. I agreed. In those days, you did things for Walt Disney that you didn't do for anyone else.

This was on location in a western North Carolina state park which was overrun with tourists who came and went at will. As I sat in a director's chair having my brow doctored, a tourist approached. He was fat, had a Brooklyn accent, and a half-chewed cigar in his mouth. He aimed his 8mm camera at me and commanded, "Hey, Bud! Move a little closer to the makeup man, will ya! I'm shootin' color, an' from here that looks like real blood."

The genius and eccentricities of Walt Disney have been the source of many anecdotes. The following is my favorite:

The Davy Crockett company was three weeks over schedule on a one-week show, with probably another week to go. Director Norman Foster was sweating over the lost schedule. Then word came that Walt was on his way to visit the set. The night before he arrived, Norman made the rounds saying goodbye to everyone. He reasoned that the boss would be introducing a new director.

Even though delays might be traced to bad planning, rough location sites, poor organization and such, when a film racks up a 400 percent overrun, it's not unusual that some heads will roll. And Norman assumed, logically, that his would be the first.

An electric quiver of anticipation invaded the set the following morning. When the long, black Cadillac was sighted approaching down the dusty country road, Norman was setting up the last shot before lunch. Whispers went from mouth to mouth: "He's here . . . Walt's here."

Walt was accompanied by Mrs. Disney and a couple from a nearby resort town who were their hosts. A welcoming scene was played behind Norman while he was acting unconcerned—acting totally unaware that possible doom was approaching. When Walt reached Norman's side, he stood for a moment and observed him busily directing.

"Hello, Norm," he said.

Norman turned and greeted surprisedly, "Oh, hello, Walt." They shook hands. "I heard you were coming." Then to fill a lull Norm said, "How does the stuff look?"

"OK," Walt said. "Except for one thing."

Uh-oh, Norman thought. Here it comes.

"You know that scene where Fess wrestles with the bear?" Walt asked.

"Yes," Norman nodded.

"I want you to retake that scene," Walt said. "That bear's zipper was showing."

Walt turned and, while our gaping-mouthed director just stared, got into his car and headed back to California.

Chapter 14

HEADIN' INTO THE HILLS

When Davy Crockett was last seen at the Alamo, he was upright and very much alive, swinging "ol' Betsy" by the barrel, and viciously braining Santa Anna's bayonet-wielding soldiers right and left.

Many nodded their heads and commented on how smart Disney was. He was leaving the door open for a sequel. How little they knew Walt. He resisted all persuasion and temptation with a simple statement: "No, that story's been told," and moved along to tell other stories. It was a mark of the innate quality and integrity of the man. Some people just call it "class."

Having been established as a "buckskin" actor in the Crockett adventures, I got a call from MGM. They had once done the Kenneth Roberts story, *Northwest Passage*, starring

JED CLAMPETT, DEFENDER OF THE HEARTH. 1962

Spencer Tracy, and now were thinking of it as a television series. Adrian Samish had been assigned as producer, and there was the part of Hunk Mariner originally played by Walter Brennan. They wanted me for this role. Keith Larsen was to play the Tracy part, Don Burnett, the role of Langdon Towne.

Of the many built-in minuses that conspire to make a project a failure, some can be detected at the start. Others are revealed as unpleasant surprises along the way. I think the MGM brass was overly impressed and misled by the left-over footage of a spectacular raid on an Abenakee Indian village. It made for a strong first episode, but the action diminished sharply thereafter. This was foreseeable. But the unpleasant surprise, concealed and discovered later, would have required a clairvoyant to anticipate.

In the mid-50s, color television was uncommon. In our stories, the "good guys" were the English in red coats, and their adversaries, the French, were in blue. On existing TV sets, both colors came out gray. As is the case with Westerns, had we been able to put the good guys in white hats and the heavies in black, the situation might have been cured. But in that era, the military hats of both sides were black. The viewer confusion over which side to root for was not helped by the show's initial time slot opposite "Maverick," which was at the peak of its popularity. Our premiere rating was a seven.

The two things I remember vividly about "Northwest Passage" involved what then seemed like a brush with death and a matchless moment of hilarity. The first involved an attack on a small Indian encampment. While the stunt coordinator was choreographing the action, the actors and stunt men walked through the routine by the numbers. He said something like this: "Rogers leads the attack, enters from this tree, tomahawks this Indian. Towne shoots the Indian who is about to knife me, as Rogers. I am attacked by two Indians. I kick one in the crotch and start to fling the other into the fire, when you, Mariner, charge in to help me. Got it? OK, let's walk it once."

We rehearsed the routine several times, walking it slowly, grunting for the indicated contacts. We seemed to know what we were doing, so the director said, "OK, let's try it on film. Everybody ready? Lotsa life now. Lotsa vitality! Roll 'em—Action!"

We came up to speed. Rogers attacked and tomahawked his Indian, Towne shot the Indian about to knife Rogers, and the two Indians attacked the stunt coordinator. He kicked one out of action and began to fling the second off as I charged in to help. Now, when the coordinator had said fling, I had been given no precise demonstration of what the word meant. What he actually did was to pick up the Indian by the shoulders and swing him like a golf club, 360 degrees, developing a fantastic club-head speed. At about 270 degrees, as I charged in, the Indian's heels caught me full in the chest and I went down. I thought I would never get up.

My chest and lungs seemed to have collapsed, and as I lay on the ground making horrible gasping noises, I actually thought, This is it! They pumped my arms and massaged my chest until, finally, I was breathing. They said I had just had the wind knocked out of me. Wind, hell! It felt more like my soul.

I prefer the lighter of the two stories, which is an

unscheduled hilarious classic. Keith Larsen was a wonderful guy, extremely modest and extremely cooperative. For instance, when a director gave him instructions, he followed them to the letter. He always hit his marks, and if a director programmed him to do a certain thing, that is what he did. Exactly. And not another thing. You could depend on that.

We were shooting an episode titled "Bound Women" about a shipment of women who had been sent over from the old country to America to become wives of the settlers. One of these women was Angie Dickenson, in her first film role. In the script, Angie had been kidnapped by an evil innkeeper and his wife, and she was being held in a bedroom of the inn. As Hunk Mariner, I had tried to rescue her, and had not only failed but had been captured myself. Then Rogers, played by Keith Larsen, would come to rescue us.

The director, Jacques Tournier, carefully explained that the panels of the door were made of balsa wood. Keith was to hit the door (which was solid except for the panels) with his body, then break a hole through the panel next to the lock, big enough to get his hand through, reach in, unlock the door, open it from the outside, and charge in to save us.

For some reason, the prop department had furnished only one breakaway door. There could be only one take. It had to be done perfectly the first time.

"Are there any questions?" Jaques asked. "Do you understand?" And he went through it all again. Keith understood perfectly. "Very well," the director said. "Light 'em up—and—roll!"

Unfortunately, when Keith's body hit the door, he missed the solid part and hit the balsa. His body crashed through the door, and he wound up headlong on the floor *inside* the room. Remembering precisely what the director had instructed, Keith picked himself up, carefully stepped back out through the splintered door, reached in, unlocked the door, and stepped back into the bedroom to rescue us. There was a beat of stunned silence—then an explosion of uncontrolled, hysterical laughter that wouldn't quit. A very red-faced Larsen shook his head and said, "That was dumb." Sure it was dumb, but we loved him for it. It made our day.

For the reasons I've mentioned, "Northwest Passage" bombed on television. But someone at MGM was thinking. They cut nine episodes into three features, released them in the foreign movie-theater market and recovered their money. Now that everyone has color television and cable television is starving for material, I'm surprised they haven't been run in the domestic markets. I'm sure they will be someday.

After "Northwest," I was riding pretty high and thinking seriously of a semiretirement from acting. My wife and I had bought an old rambling house on Balboa Island in Orange County, California, and I had a boat. I had always promised myself that someday I would sit down somewhere and write plays. This seemed like the time and the place.

Jimmy McHugh, my agent, did not exactly panic at the idea but said, "Before you retire, there are a couple of guys with some ideas that I promised you'd listen to."

The first guy was Grant Tinker. We had lunch at the Brown Derby, and I listened to an idea for a Western series. Jimmy and I said we'd think about it. Next came a man small in stature but with a giant talent, Paul Henning. He

PAUL HENNING, MAX BAER, JR., AND ME. 1962

had an office at General Service Studios.

Paul was born in Independence, Missouri. As a Boy Scout he experienced summer camping trips in the Ozarks where he absorbed firsthand impressions of the folks who dwelled there, and he never forgot them. He had a grandmother who actually kept a jug of corn whiskey close at hand under her bed to ward off "the reumatiz." As a youngster, he had jerked sodas as I had. Harry Truman was his regular customer. Later, Paul pursued a career as an attorney, but he just wasn't happy with that.

His first job in show business was sweeping out a small radio station in Kansas City. He wrote commercials and sang an occasional song on the air when the broadcast needed some continuity. Paul met, fell in love with, and married Ruth Barth, an attractive young lady who worked at the station.

Because Paul has a mind that instantly sees the funny side of everything, his destiny took him into the ranks of radio comedy writing. Don Quinn became aware of Paul's talent and asked him to submit a script for the "Fibber McGee and Molly Show," which Quinn was producing in Chicago. This led to a long and pleasant association. When the show moved from Chicago to California, the Hennings went with it.

In Hollywood, Paul's fresh, sparkling talent was instantly in demand. Later he wrote for Rudy Vallee's radio show, "The Dennis Day Show," and wrote for the popular "George Burns and Gracie Allen Show," making the transition from radio to television with the husband and wife comedy team. He created and wrote the "Bob Cummings Show" and also penned the feature film *Lover Come Back* which starred Rock Hudson and Doris Day.

Paul had a friend, Dick Wesson, who was half of a vaudeville comedy act, The Wesson Brothers. One day, Paul and Dick were reviewing the current shows and made the discovery that many of the successful shows of the time were built around tall men: Fess Parker as Davy Crockett, Ward Bond in "Wagon Train," Jim Arness in "Gunsmoke," etc.

"Who do we know that's tall?" Paul wondered.

Wesson answered, "Buddy Ebsen is tall."

And that began a chain of events, which led to a meeting in Henning's office at General Service Studios in October 1961; it was a momentous turning point in my career.

Until then, I had never met or seen Paul. My first impression was that of a cute little guy in casual clothes and a Tyrolean hat, who was effusively hospitable, hopping about the room seeing to everyone's comfort. The other two in the meeting were my agent and business associate, Jimmy McHugh, and the president of Filmways Television, Al Simon. Simon was to become the executive producer of the project that was put into motion that day.

After some amenities and hot coffee, Paul launched into his story. It was about a family of hillbillies: a solid-as-a-rock father, "Jed"; a beautiful daughter, "Elly May"; an inept nephew, "Jethro"; a feisty grandmother known as "Granny"; and cousin "Pearl," who was Jethro's mother.

During the entire recital, Paul never sat down. He enacted all the scenes, said the funny lines, and laughed loudest along with us because, as I soon discovered, Paul wrote for his own enjoyment. That the world loved what he wrote was the cherry on the whipped cream and a measure of his genius. He was so sensitive to comedy that when something particularly tickled him, he was prone to drop to the floor and roll helplessly, choking with laughter. I've seen him do it.

Paul was doing a sensational job of selling that day. We were all laughing and wiping tears, and then I got a chilling thought. Most of the laughs were coming as a result of Granny, Elly May, Jethro and Pearl. Jed was not funny, it seemed. Granny and Jethro *were*. Jed had an occasional dry, philosophical, or naive laugh line, but essentially he was a straight man. A guy could get lost in such a situation. The show sounded like a lot of fun, and I was supposed to be a part of it, but how could I survive in it? Then the answer came: These hillbillies were rich. Worth $35 million. If Jed could always control the money, he'd never get lost. And that is the deal I made with Paul. Jed was in charge of the riches. Always. He was the patriarch, the strong yet sentimental leader of the clan. Although the contractual salary minuet went on for some time, Paul and I had an understanding. I would do the show.

The others had not yet been cast. Bea Benaderet was a candidate for "Granny." Her competition was an actual hillbilly country entertainer named Cousin Emmy. She looked the part, all right. A few of us went to the Palomino, a country and western nightclub in North Hollywood where she was appearing. She was a riot. For a finish, she played "The Stars and Stripes Forever" on an inflated balloon. She was a great performer and perfect for "Granny," but she just couldn't act.

For Jethro, Paul had found a handsome, blonde young man named Roger Torrey; he had tremendous muscles and could act, but he had no sense of humor. One day,

Max Baer, Jr., walked onto the test stage. He was loose, irreverent, physically powerful, and he bubbled animal spirits. Two minutes of his face on the projection room screen and the part was his.

Actress Donna Douglas had played a small part in a feature Paul Henning had produced a few years prior to the "Hillbillies." With her looks and charm she collected friends and fervent fans with a mere "Hah, y'all." Although Donna had a league of technical and production people rooting for her, Paul resisted casting her as Elly May.

He favored instead, a little woodsy wildflower who was sweet and shy, the kind who might find a common language with critters. The world knows what choice was made, and I am sure Paul has never regretted it.

People continually ask me how you get a job in show business. There are many ways and many avenues. Whimsical chance woven into a gossamer-like web of possibilities, which sometimes hangs on a casually dropped word of a friend or stranger—and subject to the transient mood and fleeting memory of that recipient—can be a deciding factor in a career. On the other hand, sometimes a job comes from plowing straight ahead with determination and guts. Just that. The prerequisite, of course, is talent.

Irene Ryan was a seasoned performer who had run the gamut of show business since she was a child performing in tent shows. She used to say to me, "Buddy, you and I have been through the years of work. We've served our time and paid our dues. These young kids like Max and Donna got fame their first time out. They don't know what it is to struggle and scratch like we did."

Having learned years before not to depend on agents

or wait for the phone to ring, Irene was out beating the bushes. As she walked down the corridor of the building at Universal that housed writers, she stuck her head into every office and yelled, "Hi! Irene Ryan. Whattaya got for me today?" She had an Irish wit that got her past secretaries. She almost passed Paul Henning's office door but then thought, Oh, what the hell. . . .

To her standard opening line, Paul responded with sincere regrets.

Irene grinned, "Well, keep me in mind. Anyway, how've ya been?"

"Busy as a one-armed Scotsman in a burning restaurant eating a paid-up meal," Paul said.

Irene laughed. He studied her. She dressed smartly and well, this tiny lady.

(ABOVE) THE CLAMPETTS HAVE PLENTY OF REASONS TO BE THANKFUL. 1962

(OPPOSITE) GRANNY'S "GIANT JACKRABBIT" BROUGHT GIANT RATINGS. THIS EPISODE STILL RANKS HIGH IN THE NIELSEN LIST OF ALL-TIME, MOST-WATCHED PROGRAMS. 1962

"There's one part in this thing I'm doing, and you're much too young—still. . . ." He studied her some more. "If you want to, come over and test for it." Irene did. And that's how Irene Ryan became "Granny" and immortalized the word itself.

I'll always be grateful to Paul Henning. He created and wrote for me one of the best parts I ever had: J.D. Clampett. In addition to his gift for comedy, he was a sensitive, generous and caring person. The following story typifies Paul:

AS *NUMERO UNO* IN THE RATINGS, WE WERE RUBBING IT INTO NEWSPAPER CRITIC CECIL SMITH WHO HAD OUTSPOKENLY PREDICTED "THE BEVERLY HILLBILLIES" WOULD HAVE A SHORT LIFE. 1965

In 1968 I launched a thirty-five foot catamaran, *Polynesian Concept*. It was built to win the multihull Honolulu race. About that time, I heard rumors of new plans to shoot the "Hillbillies" in summer and fall and take our hiatus in winter and spring. The Honolulu race started from San Pedro on July 4th and took as long as two weeks, which would certainly conflict with the show's shooting schedule.

I had made no secret of my racing plans, and Paul, no doubt, had heard about them. I thought for sure we were on a collision course, but that was before I really knew Paul. We weren't seeing each other as much as we used to because he was very busy now writing scripts, not only for the "Hillbillies," but also for his other show, "Petticoat Junction," as well as overseeing "Green Acres" as its executive producer.

I was busy, too, preparing for the Trans Pacific race, still wondering when the confrontation might occur. Then one day, while in my dressing room, I got a call from Paul's office with word that he was sending over a messenger.

Uh-oh, I thought. This is it. The official notice of the change in the shooting schedule.

I began to mentally clear the deck for action and was preparing a defense of my racing plans when someone knocked on the door. I opened it, the messenger handed me an envelope, said, "From Mr. Henning," and departed. I delayed opening the envelope. I didn't want the conflict to begin. When I finally read the message it said, "Dear Buddy, would you greatly mind if we shot the 'Hillbillies' in Hawaii starting about July 15? Best regards, Paul."

It brought tears to my eyes. This kind, considerate

POLYNESIAN CONCEPT, "ROUND THE ISLAND" RACE, 1969, ISLE OF WIGHT.

HEADIN' INTO THE HILLS

GAMBOLING ON THE GREEN ON THE GROUNDS
OF PENSHURST CASTLE IN KENT, ENGLAND. 1968

HEADIN' INTO THE HILLS

man. Would I mind? I wanted to kiss him. The race meant a lot to me.

Well, as often happens in this Land of Oz, things changed, and we did not shoot in Hawaii. The plans took a 180-degree turn, and while I was sailing my catamaran to Hawaii, Paul had the rest of the Hillbillies, including the truck, flown off to England.

On July 16 at 1:00 A.M., I sailed past the searchlight-beam finish line off Diamond Head. Two days later, with the monkey pod winner's trophy under my arm, I was flying toward England.

At Heathrow Airport, I boarded a waiting helicopter.

After dodging some incoming flights, the pilot crossed the busy runways and headed us for the castle in Kent where the company was shooting.

With an ordinary road map on his knees, he followed the railroad tracks, dropping low to check his course by reading the signs on the train stations.

Thus we found our way through the fog, and he set us gently on the front lawn of Penshurst Castle to the cheers of the welcoming Hillbillies.

As I passed around the Hawaiian newspaper's glowing accounts of our win—hammy as that may have been—I never felt more like a hero.

The excitement of my arrival properly observed, the English crew lost no time in getting back to business—eating. My arrival had interrupted their morning tea.

They serve five meals on an English motion picture location: breakfast, morning tea, lunch, afternoon tea and then, a snack for the road.

Their teas are not just tea and ladyfingers, but

include soup, kippers, snorker, cold cuts, a hot dish—in short, a full meal.

Somehow the work gets done between these meals, come hell, high water, or the frequent "heavy mists."

All the sensitive equipment such as cameras and sound units have waterproof covers, and when the mist gets so heavy it blurs the lens, they just cover up and have a spot of tea until the rain stops. If there are puddles in the road where none were in the last scene, so what—it was shot in England, and that's the way it is in England.

We got along fine with the English, and I learned a lot from them. For example, I found they have a knack for covering over what at first reads like impertinence with respect.

Except for our director and unit manager we had an all-English crew, and one day the third assistant, a bright-faced twenty-year old brought me a completely different set of scene numbers for the day's shooting than the ones I had previously received and for which I had prepared.

I blew up, demanding how the hell they expected me to be ready to instantly shoot this new set of scenes.

The kid gave me a snap-on perfunctory smile and said, "With all due respect, sir—that's not my problem," and bounced off.

I was so impressed with the line that I now often use it myself.

JETHRO'S FINEST HOUR

Max Baer, Jr., with his mighty muscles and quick thinking, once saved me from serious injury. Possibly death. It happened in what might, in a sense, be described as a "helicopter crash."

In the show, during Jethro's "Double-Naught-Spy" phase, he inventively installed helicopter blades on the old Hillbilly truck, and with blind faith in the feasibility of his conversion, he and I prepared for takeoff in our first test flight.

For the shot, the truck was mounted on hydraulic jacks, the camera framed tightly only on us. As the blades overhead began to whirl, the jacks slowly raised the truck, giving the illusion on film that it was taking off.

Take One! Lights! Camera! Action! The system worked all right, until it became apparent that the designer had not cranked in the vibration factor. The whirling blades rocked the truck. At an altitude of twelve feet, they shook the truck's body right off the jacks. It began falling in my direction, so I instinctively dove out into space as far as I could, hoping to avoid the plummeting junker.

I hit the concrete sound stage floor hard and lay there dazed and befuddled from my crash landing but conscious enough to wonder why the truck hadn't landed on me. I looked upward.

And there was Max, sturdy as the Colossus of Rhodes, coolly bracing the truck above me until I was dragged to safety. How he got there so fast I can only guess. God had temporarily lent him a pair of angel's wings.

(ABOVE) THE CLAMPETTS IN THE EASTER PARADE. 1962

(OPPOSITE) FILMING IN SILVER DOLLAR CITY. 1962

(ABOVE) HEADIN' INTO THE HILLS, BEVERLY HILLS THAT IS. 1962

(BELOW) THIS IS MY FAVORITE EPISODE OF "THE BEVERLY HILLBILLIES" AND THE
FIRST ONE FILMED IN COLOR. AS ADMIRAL JED CLAMPETT, I PLAYED IT
SO CONVINCINGLY THAT I WAS RECEIVING SALUTES FROM REAL GOBS. 1962

(ABOVE) ENJOYING A JOKE WITH MY FRIEND, JOHN WAYNE, A GUEST STAR IN THE EPISODE "THE INDIANS ARE COMING." 1962

(BELOW) PHIL SILVERS, AS SHIFTY SHAFER, SELLS JED VARIOUS CHOICE PIECES OF REAL ESTATE IN WASHINGTON, DC. FROM THE EPISODE "JED BUYS THE CAPITOL." 1962

HEADIN' INTO THE HILLS

THE BEVERLY HILLBILLIES
Cast, Broadcast Data and Merits

"Wellll, Doggies!" We had a series on CBS that got America's attention like a willow switch whacking a hound dog's heinie. It was as intoxicating as an explosion of Granny's still. And it still survives. Despite depressing reviews from the beginning, the public seemed to thoroughly enjoy the adventures of the Clampett clan in Beverly Hills. It would have been interesting if we had all written down our predictions and put them in a time capsule.

Here, thirty-something years later, the Clampetts are still as much a part of Americana as apple pie. Of the current crop of programs, which do you think will survive in popularity in the year 2012, when the Hillbillies celebrate their golden anniversary? Any? I'm certainly proud to have been a part of this classic, and as Jed, I acquired the most diverting and enjoyable family I have ever known, outside of my own.

CAST

Buddy Ebsen	Jed Clampett
Irene Ryan	Granny
Max Baer, Jr.	Jethro Bodine
Donna Douglas	Elly May Clampett
Bea Benaderet	Cousin Pearl Bodine
Raymond Bailey	Milburn Drysdale
Harriet MacGibbon	Margaret Drysdale
Nancy Kulp	Miss Jane Hathaway

BROADCAST DATA

- First telecast: September 26, 1962
- Last telecast: September 7, 1971
- Shot on 35mm film, 274 episodes (106 in black and white, 168 in color) at General Service Studios
- Produced by Filmways Television, Inc.
- Created, Produced, and Written by Paul Henning (some episodes were written with other individuals)
- Theme song: "The Ballad of Jed Clampett" Words and music by Paul Henning

MERITS

- "The Beverly Hillbillies" shot to the number one spot quicker than any other program in television history. By the third episode they were America's favorite.

- "The Beverly Hillbillies'" highest rated episode aired January 8, 1964, and altered television history when it received a 44 percent rating and a 65 percent market share. To this day, that one show remains the highest rated half-hour sitcom since 1960 when Nielsen changed their rating system.

- Unlike any other television show, "The Beverly Hillbillies" claims 19 entries in Nielsen's Top 100 list of the all-time highest rated programs.

- In 1992, the program was still syndicated in thirty-five countries and could be seen in some parts of the United States four times a day.

- During its nine-year run, the show played host to such celebrities as John Wayne, Phil Silvers, Gloria Swanson, Roy Clark, Sammy Davis, Jr., Hedda Hopper, Arthur Treacher, Eva Gabor, Don Rickles, and Charles Ruggles.

THE LEGEND OF "THE BEVERLY HILLBILLIES" THIRTY YEARS LATER—
IT HIT NUMBER 4 IN THE NIELSEN RATINGS. 1993

BARNABY JONES

Two events in 1971 considerably altered the course of my career: First, one hour of CBS programming fell out, ratings-wise, and became an immediate candidate for replacement. Second, at that time I was booked as a guest star on the show "Cannon," which starred William Conrad and was produced by Quinn Martin.

One day my agent Jimmy McHugh appeared on the set of "Terror at 39,000 Feet," a movie of the week in which I was working. He mysteriously pulled me over to an isolated corner of the stage and said in low tones, "Don't tell this to a soul, not even your wife." Then, before continuing, he furtively looked around.

"Tell what?" I asked.

"Freddie Silverman has decided that instead of your

being a guest on the 'Cannon' series, Cannon will be a guest on the first episode of *your* new series."

Silverman was in charge of programming for CBS. His name gave me bad vibes; after all, he had been responsible for canceling the "Hillbillies." And his idea, when I grasped it, was a little mind-boggling.

"No pilot?" was my first thought.

"You'll use the same script," Jimmy explained. "Silverman wants thirteen episodes—now!"

The existing script had detective Barnaby emerging from retirement to avenge the murder of his son with the help of Cannon; then Barnaby would resume a career as a private eye. As an episode of "Cannon," the script was structured as a possible spin-off, but it was a spin-off *before* exposure. A bold gamble. It was one more private-eye story in a saturated market. Would the viewers buy it? I really had my doubts.

"I won't tell anybody," I said.

Next morning, driving to work, I was listening to my favorite morning radio man, Dick Whittinghill. "Guess who's going to have his own TV show next season?" he asked listeners. "Buddy Ebsen. You know—Jed Clampett." So much for secrecy in the Land of Oz.

I was assigned a dressing room suite and parking space on the Goldwyn lot. Two days later, an attractive young lady parked her station wagon nearby, got out, and approached me, smiling. "We've never met," she said. "I'm Lee Meriwether. I'm your new daughter-in-law." This former Miss America who had made a go of an acting career was referring, of course, to the role she had just won in the series. Her appearance was soft, feminine, belied by a strong, firm handshake. The skin texture spoke of a girl who works. This lady, I concluded, does her own gardening.

Except for one miserable, rainy and cold 4:00 A.M. shooting session down among the San Pedro docks, the filming went smoothly. Bill Conrad was easy to work with and hospitably shared his motor home with me, since I was the new boy and had yet to be assigned one.

While setting up the last, or "wrap" shot, director Walter Grauman studied me quizzically. He was a veteran. He was Quinn Martin's favorite director and had been with him since "The Untouchables."

"I don't know," he mused. "This show has got every *cliché*, every gimmick that's ever been on any other PI show. There's nothing new in it. I don't know why anyone would want to watch it. Except for one thing," he grinned. "People like you."

"Thanks, Walter," I said. "I hope you're right."

Selecting a name for the show took some doing. Barnaby as a first name was set. Choices for the last name had been whittled to two: "Flint" or "Cobb," heaven forbid. I objected to Cobb. "Why give the reviewers a setup?" Quinn agreed. So for a time it was Barnaby Flint. One day in Quinn's office we were discussing Barnaby's character. "I see him as sort of a foxy grandpa," he said.

I didn't.

"How do you see him?"

Searching for the words, I said, "I see him as a cool, methodical human being; a shrewd judge of character engaged in the sometimes routine, sometimes exciting business of catching crooks." Quinn absently nodded.

"Play him your way," he said.

I could see his mind was far away. Then he blurted out the name. "Jones!"

"What?"

"How 'bout Jones? Barnaby Jones?"

It had an agreeable ring to it. "Why not?" I said. And a new television character was christened.

A few months later we were shooting our sixth show in a private home in Bel Air when the phone rang. It was Quinn. "He wants to talk to you," the assistant said as he handed me the phone.

"You want to hear the numbers?" he asked.

We had premiered the evening before, and he was referring to the overnight ratings.

"*You* tell *me*. Do I want to hear them?"

"I think you do," he said. "'Barnaby Jones,' seventeenth; *Lawrence of Arabia*, thirty-seventh."

Lawrence of Arabia had been our competition, a theatrical blockbuster which was airing for the first time on television.

"That's encouraging," I said.

"*Encouraging*? It's a wipeout! We won the hour!" he sputtered.

With the word out, the mood on the set instantly became a celebration. Electricians, carpenters, soundmen and crew workers are just as sensitive to the ratings as the producers, stars and network presidents. A smash television show means sustained employment. The term in show business is "going to heaven."

But despite the auspicious debut, reviewers found little to praise in "Barnaby Jones." In a world dominated by "Columbo," "Kojak," "Mannix," "McCloud," "Cannon," and "McMillan and Wife," our show was dismissed as just one more cop show. They discounted the strong premiere against *Lawrence of Arabia* as a fluke and predicted "Barnaby's" disappearance from the tube in just a matter of weeks. Just as in the case of "The Beverly Hillbillies," the ratings confounded and annoyed the critics. The show played out its original thirteen weeks, bouncing about among the first ten or twenty in the ratings with a healthy audience.

Although "Barnaby" was perceived and fixed in the minds of the network brass as merely a thirteen-week replacement, the ratings by the end of the first half-season were of such substance that they were afraid to cancel it. Hedging, they purchased another twenty-three episodes.

During an affiliates' meeting at the Beverly Hills Hotel at the start of the third season, Freddie Silverman invited me to sit down at his table for a drink. He complimented me on the surprising success of the show, then, fixing me with a meaningful stare, he raised his glass and said, *"Enjoy this year."* His words conveyed a message that could be perceived only one way: For "Barnaby," this would be the last year. So after gulping and accepting his pronouncement with some regret, I enjoyed a third year. I also enjoyed a fourth and a fifth and a sixth and seventh and even an eighth; I'm also enjoying the residuals from syndicated reruns.

Meanwhile, back at the networks, playing the game of executive musical chairs, Silverman switched from CBS to a hungry network, ABC, where he set out to knock off the ratings of his former employer. But no matter what he threw against "Barnaby Jones," nothing made a dent.

RESEARCHING "BARNABY JONES," I VISITED THE
LOS ANGELES COUNTY SHERIFF'S FORENSIC FACILITIES. 1971

"Barnaby" just went on and on. Each year, as they appraised the fall lineups, the prophecies included lines like "the aging 'Barnaby Jones' will probably not last the season," or "the fading 'Barnaby Jones' is a likely candidate for mid-season replacement."

I'm not sure who came up with it, but Barnaby was given a penchant for drinking milk. It wasn't that he disapproved of people who drink alcohol, it was just that he liked milk. It became his trademark.

During a hiatus, I was sailing my boat off the West Coast of Florida. I went into a little restaurant in Pensacola, sat a moment, then a young waitress with a big grin on her face walked over and put a glass of milk on my table. It was a win-win situation. She enjoyed the gag. I enjoyed the milk—plus the recognition. It happens quite often now.

Meanwhile, Freddie Silverman moved along to NBC. His hot hand seemed to be cooling. For whatever reasons, a series of disappointing projects fed rumors of a crack in his infallibility. The speculations as to his future were finally resolved when he was replaced by Grant Tinker. Obviously, Freddie Silverman's once skyrocketing star was definitely descending.

It was during this time that I was flown east to do some promos for "Barnaby" which were being shot against typical New York backgrounds. On this particular morning we were working in front of the Plaza Hotel. I was having my makeup repaired at the Fifth Avenue entrance, when I noticed a small covey of businessmen, carrying briefcases, approaching from Fifty-Ninth Street. The short one in the center looked familiar. As the others passed into the hotel, he approached me. With a wry grin and a sense of humor that will forever endear him to me, he said, "Remember me? I'm Freddie Silverman."

"How could I forget," I said, shaking his hand warmly. "*You* put me in business."

RON HOWARD

Here is the way the ball sometimes bounces in Hollywood.

Before I found a seventeen-year bonanza of continuous employment in "The Beverly Hillbillies" and "Barnaby Jones," I made guest appearances on a lot of television series. One such was "The Andy Griffith Show," where I played a shiftless drifter who befriends Opie Taylor (in the episode, "Opie's Hobo Friend"). One of the key elements in the show's success was that bright little redheaded kid.

Everyone was impressed with Ronny Howard, as was I. I was also impressed with his parents and the cool, intelligent way they had done their part; there was nothing of a spoiled brat about him.

The next time our paths crossed we were in a 1981

I KNEW THIS KID WHEN HE WAS A KID. 1981

television movie of the week, "Fire on the Mountain," a Johnny Carson Production for NBC. Ron was now quite grownup. He and I costarred in this movie, where I portrayed a rancher who decided to fight back when the government attempted to take his land for a missile base expansion program. Ron played a money-hungry young man whose values slowly changed until he finally sided with me. Ron and I got along very well working together, and we often reminisced about Mayberry.

While we made the picture, Ron was spending a lot of his time between shots carrying a video camera and interviewing people.

Little did anyone suspect that this activity may have been part of his preparation for a major transition from actor to director.

His directorial smash hit was *Splash* in 1984, a charming fantasy about a mermaid.

Something seismic happens when an artist is suddenly a major success in Hollywood. Not so much that it brings about a change in the artist, but it sure makes a difference in the world's attitude toward him or her. Suddenly all doors are open and everything previously unattainable seems to become attainable. The phone rings incessantly, and friends you never knew you had come running. If you are a real friend, however, you never crowd in at a time like this.

I was thrilled at Ron's success, proud that I had worked with him, and I went about my business.

I was totally unprepared for the phone call I got one day from Jimmy McHugh.

"Ron Howard called today," he told me. "He wants to talk to you."

"What about?" I asked.

"A part in his new picture, *Cocoon*."

The news was thrilling.

Fate sure knows how to torture a fellow. Here I was, locked into a year with the television series, "Matt Houston," and the hottest director in town calls to talk about a part in his next project. I don't wish to disparage television or "Matt Houston" or its star, Lee Horsley—a true gentleman and friend. But a part in the new Ron Howard feature? For the big screen? Wow!

But a sad fact remained: I was unavailable, so the part went to Don Ameche. Don made the most of it and won an Academy Award. And even though he got what might have been mine, Don Ameche will always receive my highest marks as a talented gentleman of rare humor and humility.

He afforded me a wry, bittersweet chuckle when, at a public acceptance speech, he reportedly said: "I want to thank my mother, I want to thank my father. . . . I want to thank my agent, and I want to thank Ron Howard. Also, I want to thank Buddy Ebsen for being unavailable to play the part."

Chapter

17

FILMS, TELEVISION & STAGE

The Girl of the Golden West (1938)

Broadway Melody of 1936 (1935)
Captain January (1936)
Born to Dance (1936)
Banjo on My Knee (1936)
Broadway Melody of 1938 (1937)
Yellow Jack (1938)

Parachute Battalion (1941)

Night People (1954)

My Lucky Star (1938)
Four Girls in White (1939)
The Kid from Texas (1939)
They Met in Argentina (1941)
Sing Your Worries Away (1942)
The Hanging Judge (1942)

Red Garters (1954)

Attack (1956)

Under Mexicali Stars (1950)
Utah Wagon Train (1951)
Rodeo King and the Señorita (1951)
Silver City Bonanza (1951)
Thunder in God's Country (1951)
Davy Crockett (1955)

The Interns (1962)

Mail-Order Bride (1964)

Davy Crockett and the River Pirates (1956)
Fragile Fox (1955)
Between Heaven and Hell (1956)
Breakfast at Tiffany's (1961)
The Beverly Hillbillies (1993)

The One And Only, Original Family Band (1968)

WORKING IN GERMANY

When I made *Night People* in Germany with Gregory Peck, the director was an old friend, Nunnally Johnson, who had written and produced *Banjo On My Knee,* in which I had appeared some years earlier.

Like most Hollywood "hyphenates," being human, Nunnally had succumbed to the vanity of being a triple-threat hyphenate, writer-producer *and* director, and though he had never directed a picture before he had convinced Darrell Zanuck, the head Wizard at Twentieth Century-Fox, that he could direct.

Taking advantage of the still war-torn look of Berlin in 1954, we shot the exteriors there, then moved down to Munich to Geisel Gestag Studios to shoot the interiors.

One morning I walked onto the set rather early and found Nunnally alone, seated in his director's chair, his glasses on his forehead, his script on his lap, and a very puzzled look on his face.

He didn't speak, so I watched as he referred repeatedly to various pages of the script, making vague motions with his hand as though visualizing actors entering, exiting, and generally moving about in the set.

Finally, he slapped his hand down disgustedly on his script.

In his soft Georgia accent he said, "You know—Ah'm a goddamned fool."

To my startled look, he continued, "When Ah was just a writah-producer, Ah could *hiah* some idiot to make this crap work."

Despite all the exigencies of learning how, I found

Nunnally to be an excellent director, a delight to work with because he never lost his sense of humor.

The evening my cab pulled up at my destination, the new Kimkinski Hotel on the Kurfurstsudam in Berlin, I was twenty-four hours and three plane changes from L.A. Nunnally and his unit manager Gerd Oswald were finishing brandy and coffee at the sidewalk cafe in front of the hotel. Spying me, Nunnally insisted I send my bags up and join them in the waiting limousine to drive down to the shooting location where the scene was being set up and lit for the next shot. I acquiesced.

When we arrived at the location, a spooky bombed-out area next to the Berlin wall—now ablaze with arc lights—I heard Nunnally moan an, "Oh no! Goddamn it, Ah told Horstle *'against the wall'*—do these Germans really understand English?" He leapt from the car to confront his assistant director.

Apparently Nunnally had wanted to shoot the scene against the Berlin wall and was dismayed to find the lights concentrated on the side of a bombed-out house 180-degrees in the opposite direction.

Horstle quietly explained, "You see the soldier on the wall with the Tommy gun?" pointing out the ominous silhouette. "Well, the next time one of these arc lights shines in his eyes, he says he will shoot it out."

Nunnally's instant switch was comic in its swiftness. "That's what Ah say," he ordered, "shoot it against the house."

One day we were in the studio sound stage in Munich trying to film a very quiet scene, but we were stymied by a persistent hammering sound. Nunnally cut the action and addressed his first assistant, who was standing at his side. "Please, could we stop that hammerin'?" Instantly the air exploded with that worthy's bellowing voice: *"Ruhe! Ruhe! Absolute Ruhe!"* The command was picked up spontaneously and repeated by the second assistant standing on the periphery of the action, *"Ruhe! Ruhe! Absolute Ruhe!"* This cued a third assistant some distance away to sound off for *"Ruhe,"* and a fourth voice even more distant and out of sight to pick up and extend the command out into and down the street.

As the sound stage echoed with this cacophony of the continuous commands for silence, Nunnally quietly raised his hand. "Please," he said. "Could we just have the hammerin'! It's much quietah than all this 'roo-ah.'"

German efficiency is a sterling quality, often carried to degrees beyond belief.

It was the prescribed duty of the makeup artist at Geisel Gestag Studios not only to make up each actor's face—but also to cut his hair—not once a week or whenever it seemed to need it, but *every morning!*

I was playing an American Army sergeant with a close-cropped crewcut. The argument that my hair would not have grown perceptibly overnight mattered not at all to the makeup artist. He believed that in the normal processes of nature—it must have—so he cut it!

Lest you feel I disapprove of this inbred universal Teutonic religion of thoroughness, please note and accept this disavowal: I get along fine with Germans—in fact, I married one.

And should you get the impression it was all work and no play in Germany, let me hasten to assure you there were "happy hours."

One evening after shooting, Gregory Peck and I were relaxing over a couple of steins of foaming lager in the Munich Hofbrau Haus.

After the second refill we fell to discussing the business we were in—acting—and I learned from him, without probing, one of the innermost technical secrets of Peck's consistent success.

"It's my 'neutral look,'" he said.

"Your what?" I asked—and he went into detail.

"Sometimes when I am playing a highly dramatic scene, lengthy, with a lot of emotional ups and downs, the camera moves in on me for a big head close-up. That's when I give them my neutral look."

"Your neutral look?" I questioned. "And how do you achieve that?"

"I don't think of anything. I just make my mind a complete blank—and the audience reads into that look whatever they are feeling—so they say, "What an actor! He made me feel exactly what he was thinking."

"Which was nothing."

Peck nodded, grinned and took another sip of his beer. "It works—try it sometime."

I have, but I'm afraid it's a technique that works only for Greg.

It was 1954, and although the fighting was over, there were many American troops stationed in Germany, all requesting personal appearances and/or entertainment from those of us in the *Night People* company, who possessed live-performance capability.

We put together a show which was mostly Max

Showalter and me, with Max at the piano while I sang and danced.

These experiences were sometimes bizarre, sometimes amusing, but always educational.

Augsburg, near Munich, was a military base with a veteran combat colonel in charge.

He was bursting with pride over the new Quonset hut he had constructed as a "theater," to house appearances such as ours for the entertainment of the troops.

There was, however, only one entrance to his theater and that was through the front door. So we trooped in and down the center aisle onto the stage, in full view of the raucously enthusiastic GIs.

The show was well received, but not as effectively as it might have been, had there been a stage door for us to enter privately, affording more anticipation and impact to each individual appearance.

Later at the Officers' Club I had a drink with the colonel, and he was looking for compliments.

"How do you like our setup?" he asked.

"Fine," I said, "except for one thing."

He looked slightly crestfallen.

"Colonel," I said, "what is the most important word in military strategy?"

He thought a moment, then answered, "Surprise."

"Exactly," I said, "it's the same in show business."

A great light seemed to dawn on him. The next day he cut a stage door into his theater.

While in Munich, Max Showalter and I were asked to perform for patients in a military hospital ward. We were mindful that the military situation in Germany was still serious

(Berlin was ringed by Russian armor), and border clashes were common.

Even though there were only seven patients in the ward, Max and I were zealously dedicated to entertaining these wounded heroes with our best tender loving care.

When we had finished our performance and were preparing to go from bed to bed, to chat with each man individually, and perhaps to get his stateside home phone number, so we could call his folks when we returned, I asked an attendant what the seven were being treated for.

He said, "Oh, two of them for broken legs in skiing accidents, one got drunk and fell off an Army truck, and the rest have the clap."

But the most rewarding experience in this live performing phase of our German experience was a show we did for East German refugees.

It happened in a large school classroom in Berlin.

There was a raised platform at one end of the room, supporting an untuned piano.

The room was packed with people: some individuals and some entire families from all strata of the East German population.

They had made perilous escapes, past armed guards and attack dogs, across a no-man's-land border, taking with them only their small portable treasures, their toothbrushes, and the clothes on their backs.

They were held in a refugee pool in Berlin, prior to being flown West to receptive friends, relatives or sympathizers, for assimilation into a kinder, gentler society.

In spite of the necessary abandonment of nearly all their material possessions, they were the happiest audience I

ever played to.

Berlin's situation was precarious. We were ringed by overwhelming Russian armor, which could have taken the city at will, but these people were enjoying, for the moment, no matter what the cost, the euphoria of just breathing the air of this island of freedom in a menacing sea of tyranny.

It was a moving lesson to us Americans—who take our heroically won privileges for granted.

WITH RITA GAM AND GREGORY PECK IN *NIGHT PEOPLE,*
MADE IN GERMANY. 1953

The Daughters Of Joshua Cabe (1972)

MADE-FOR-TELEVISION MOVIES

The President's Plane is Missing (1971)
Tom Sawyer (1973)
The Horror at 37,000 Feet (1973)
Smash-Up on Interstate 5 (1976)
Leave Yesterday Behind (1978)
The Critical List (1978)
The Bastard (miniseries, 1978)
The Paradise Connection (1979)
Return of the Beverly Hillbillies (1981)
Fire on the Mountain (1981)
Stone Fox (1987)
Working Trash (1990)

WORKING IN CANADA

I have played Toronto, and I have played Montreal on stage and in a nightclub: both times were in winter, and both times there was snow.

Both places are just across our northern border in southern Canada. So when I was hired for a picture to be made in Edmonton, Canada, in December, in a latitude several hundred miles north of the border, I had every reason to expect snow—probably blizzards.

The producers of the picture, encouraged by the weather man, also had this expectation of snow; in fact, since the story was about a dogsled race, they knew they would be sunk without it.

Following is the account of how close they came to being sunk:

A production schedule is basically divided into two categories of sets: interior and exterior. The prudent moviemaker will always shoot the exteriors first, for insurance against the possibility of inclement weather. The interiors are called "cover sets" to be fallen back on in the event of rain or, in this case, lack of snow.

When I arrived in Edmonton the first week in December, it was so cold it hurt to take a deep breath. But, no snow—so we plunged into the interiors.

Three things impressed me: the ingratiating warmth of the Canadians; the expertise of the crew, which somehow you don't expect to find away from Hollywood; and the sensitivity and protectiveness of our director, Harvey Hart.

Some directors permit the crew to drive nails, dress the set and drag lights around while the actors are rehearsing. Not so Harvey Hart. There was no softness about the way he would take over. He would chase out the crew, and the entire stage would be made as quiet as if the camera were rolling before he would begin to direct a rehearsal.

The story we were shooting concerned a Wyoming rancher in failing health; his twelve-year-old grandson, who in the course of the story must shed his childhood and grow up enough to shoulder the responsibilities of the ranch; the boy's dog, that becomes a pivotal character in the dogsled race; and "Stone Fox," a troublesome Indian for whom the picture is named.

I made one stupid mistake in preparing for this job. I figured a Wyoming cattle rancher should wear cowboy boots, so I brought a pair of mine along and wore them.

They worked fine in the interior sequences, but once they had been established on film as my foot gear, I was stuck with them outside in sub-zero temperatures. We'll go into that later.

The unit manager of the company was a charming and efficient Englishman named Peter Thompson.

We hit it off well, and had many afterwork happy hour drinks together, but as each day's shooting ate into the backlog of cover sets, and not one snowflake fell, the happy hours got less and less happy.

On the day we finished the last interior shot, Peter glumly moved the company to the exterior ranch location, about an hour's drive west of Calgary, and prayed for the snow the weather man had half-promised.

After we waited two snowless days in a dreary little motel at the foot of the Rockies, Peter made an executive decision: he shut down the company, and I found myself back home in Long Beach to enjoy Christmas and New Year's with Dorothy.

Called back in January on the rumor of snow, I took Dorothy back with me for luck, also for warmth on those cold Canadian nights. But still no snow.

Peter's next move was to abandon the existing ranch set and build a new corral, barn and cabin, higher up in the Rockies where it always snowed. Always that is—except this time.

After two more days of waiting and with the wires from the front office getting hotter, Peter, in desperation, commandeered all the largest trucks in the area, sent them up above the timber line where there was *beaucoup* snow on the ground, and began loading and shuttling them back and forth to the ranch set until it was beautifully snowbound.

So all of Peter's troubles were over? *Of course not!* That night we had a *blizzard,* and it took the snowplows half a day to clear off enough snow so we could shoot. "Peter," I told him, "out of the richness of my experience, I am going to give you three words that will describe for all time, a day in the motion picture business."

"And they are?" Peter asked.

"It's never nothing."

"Say it again—I want to write that down."

Looking around as the work began, I noticed everyone in the company was wearing proper snow boots except me. They were a sort of hi-tech, rubber, soft-lined Eskimo boot, with ample room to accommodate chemical heaters. These chemical heaters were marvelous little bags of an unknown-to-me chemical which, when activated with one bag at your toes and one under your instep, would keep your tootsies toasty in the deepest snow.

My cowhide cowboy boots were mere cold conductors; they sponged up moisture and were too tight to accommodate the chemical heaters without great discomfort.

I was in real danger of losing toes to frostbite if I stayed out in the snow too long.

"What a dummy," I berated myself: A Wyoming rancher *could* have snow boots.

The crisis came late one afternoon. I had been on-camera most of the day, without the usual breaks to go to the dressing room, get my boots off, and thaw out my toes.

The company was working in a field three-feet-deep in snow. I had finished the wide shots of a scene in which I fork hay from my wagon sled to my starving cattle. As I do so I overexert myself, suffer a stroke and collapse on the bed of the wagon. My grandson rushes to me in a panic, and tries to help. Semiconscious, I must play a close-up scene with him as I lie there. I have now had the boots on for three hours, and have no feeling at all in my toes and very little in my feet.

Harvey Hart, the soul of compassion, would love to send me to the dressing room to warm up, but the sun is going down and he *must* have this shot.

"Take his boots off," he commands.

Two darling girls, one from makeup, the other from wardrobe, comply.

"Set the camera here." Harvey indicates a spot three feet from my shoes that won't include my feet. "Rub his feet, somebody." Both girls are already doing it. "Lights—Camera—Action!"

Ten minutes later I was in my dressing room, my feet

in hot water and feeling better, but strange things were happening to the rest of me.

I was shaking violently and uncontrollably, and when I closed my eyes I saw the color red with what looked like a blizzard of snowflakes floating around in it.

The First Assistant Director popped his head in to see how I was, noted my symptoms, and said, "Let's get him down off the hill."

Soon, still shaking, I was bundled into a car for my hourlong drive to the hotel. There Dorothy got me some hot soup, into a hot tub, and around a hot toddy.

I felt much better, well enough to again tell her the whole story.

At the mention of the red-blizzard vision she said, "You had hypothermia—that can be very dangerous." "Oh," I said. Dorothy studied me closely a moment, and then said, "Now, tell me again about the girls who rubbed your feet."

WITH MY INFAMOUS COWBOY BOOTS AND GORDON TOO TOOSIS WHO PLAYED "STONE FOX," THE INDIAN IN THE FILM OF THE SAME NAME. 1986

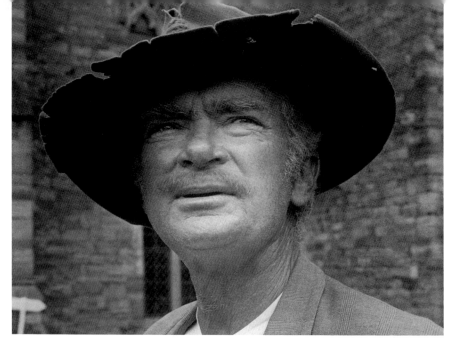

The Beverly Hillbillies (1962-1971)

TELEVISION: AS A REGULAR

The Adventures of Davy Crockett (1954-1955)
Barnaby Jones (1973-1980)
Matt Houston (1984-1985)

Northwest Passage (1958-1959)

TELEVISION APPEARANCES

Gruen
Guild Playhouse
Broadway Television Theatre
Schlitz Playhouse of Stars
Climax!
Playhouse 90
Black Saddle
Rawhide
Johnny Ringo
Maverick
GE Theatre
Riverboat
Cheyenne
Gunsmoke
77 Sunset Strip
The Twilight Zone
The Andy Griffith Show
Have Gun, Will Travel
Bus Stop
Adventures in Paradise
Highways of Melody
The Danny Kaye Show
Hollywood Palace
Art Linkletter's House Party
The Cowsills Special
Jimmy Durante Presents
Hollywood Television

Hawaii Five-O
Bonanza
Night Gallery
Alias Smith and Jones
The Tonight Show
Starring Johnny Carson
The Mac Davis Show
Tiny Tree

Carousel

The Best Man

WORKING IN MEXICO

Once upon a time I made a movie in Mexico.

I believe the producer's name was Eddie Lewis. It was the first picture for Robert Aldrich as a director, debuting his climb to the very top of his profession. The writer was Luther Davis, a respectable word-craftsman; Johnny Mercer, a top songwriter, completed the creative roster of the project.

It was probably the worst picture ever made; so bad it was funny. Today I wish I had a copy, but after trying recently to find a print, I suspect a successful and affluent Bob Aldrich acquired and destroyed them all to protect his reputation.

The picture was called *The Pussyfootin' in Rocks*, for reasons I will reveal later.

I played two parts—twins—though I only got one salary. I was the "straight-arrow" lawman hero, and also the "dirty dog" villain.

A character actress named Kathryn—I forget her last name—played the leader of a masked band of desperadoes who, when finally unmasked, all had her face. They were all called by their family name, "The Ripplehissians."

I will describe the plot, then let you decide what exotic substance the writers were on when they wrote it.

I—as the dirty dog villain—was engaged in the nefarious trade of smuggling illegal aliens into the country. These aliens were easily identified as to country, being attired in their various traditional national clothing. The Germans were in *lederhosen*, the Dutch wore wooden shoes, the English were in tweeds and monocles, and so on.

To conceal themselves as they crossed the border, each carried a piece of camouflage-painted tarpaulin, to crouch under when threatened with discovery. This move, done simultaneously on signal, created a startling comic effect, as a landscape apparently strewn with boulders advanced on the beholder intermittently—hence the title, *The Pussyfootin' in Rocks*.

I, as the straight-arrow lawman, acted to thwart this scam of my wicked brother, since his double dastardly doings called for disposing of all evidence of crime by having his henchmen, the Ripplehissians, dispatch their incredibly gullible aliens with a knock on the head and a drop into a deep well.

My girlfriend, played by Joan Blondell, stands by her man through the twists and turns of this malodorous melodrama, and our romance survives complications and misunderstandings stemming from my twin-ship and finally triumphs as we make the world a better place for everyone through our apprehension and incarceration of my wicked twin. So much for the plot.

My path to Mexico City was sprinkled with strange and disquieting omens.

Aviacion Mexicali, or some such company, painted their planes white. This made for an eye-catching contrast to the small, very black rivulet of oil leaking across the wing from the port engine of the plane I was boarding.

You became aware of this situation just as your foot hit the first step of the boarding ladder. This fascinating discovery held up the line a beat, as each passenger's mind crash-processed the following message: Oh, oh—I don't want to get on this airplane—but, if I don't, all these people behind me will think I'm chicken. Oh, what the hell—today I'm a fatalist. (Then you board.)

Surprisingly, the plane held together and took us to Mexico City, where a full mariachi band, five guitars and two trumpets, greeted us. Apparently playing for me personally, they followed my every footstep, playing me into the men's room, the baggage claim area and customs.

My then-wife believed the food in Mexico to be inedible, so she had packed me provisions. They consisted of sandwiches packaged neatly in a rectangular shape and stowed in my suitcase.

It wasn't until the customs inspector displayed an undue interest in this item that the thought occurred to me: It *did* look a lot like a neatly wrapped package of currency.

The man pointed to it, "What's that?"

"My lunch," I said, returning his stare. He gave me a look I can only describe as reproachfully disbelieving. I think it was the timely arrival of the suave and worldly Luther Davis to pay off the band and more or less take charge, that changed everything.

The customs man considered.

He could have cleared me by simply opening the package—which he had not touched. But he must have known that sometimes it is not profitable to nose about in the business affairs of men with obvious "connections" to other men of apparent consequence. He closed my bag and passed me through.

Our ride to the hotel was uneventful except where traffic was held up for troop movements in full battle gear. I checked with Luther to see if there were any revolutions scheduled—he didn't know of any, but "you never can tell."

After settling in at the posh hotel, I caught up with Joan Blondell, who had arrived the day before.

Early the next morning we were driven to the studio some distance out of town, by an eighteen-year-old driver, and got our first taste of the local driving styles. In Mexico City there are foot-deep potholes in all the streets. Nobody drives any slower, however, guaranteeing that every car, no matter how new, has broken springs and snubbers, and the passengers have spinal problems.

On the forty-five-minute drive to the studio the thrills began.

It was a two-lane highway with a white line down the middle, heavy with truck traffic. Heading up a hill behind a laboring truck, our driver got impatient and started to pass. We were straddling the centerline when an approaching eighteen-wheeler came into view over the rise, barreling straight at us.

I yelled, "Look out!" Joan shrieked—but the kid just floored it, and we squeezed by, three abreast, sandwiched between these two monsters. Our driver, once in the clear, swung over into the right-hand lane before he looked around at us, puzzled, to see what all the fuss was about.

It was then I realized, *This is the way they drive here all the time!*

Joan was in shock and clutching at straws, and noting the Virgin Mary figure dangling from his rear-view mirror, she screamed, "Tell him I'm pregnant!" When you don't speak the language, this condition is difficult to pantomime, especially from the back seat to a manic driver—but I tried.

My first day before the camera, I was driven to the location set at 7:30 A.M., but there was no camera.

As my four-wheel-drive jeep went bumping down the rocky hill from this goat country in which I had been deposited, I looked around and saw Bob Aldrich and Luther Davis sitting on a rock. I joined them.

They had been waiting there an hour for the *company* to join them.

My arrival was encouraging because Bob's mood was verging on helpless despair, expressed in bursts of suppressed sardonic laughter. This was his first day on his first directing job, and from his wide experience as a top AD or first assist on many movies, he knew better than most that this was a bad way to start a picture. The distant "front office" people are never interested in your problems—only results—and for an over-budget picture, the director is always to blame.

In Mexican production, at that time, the rules and regulations covering movie work almost defied you to succeed. For instance, you were allowed to bring only leading players and a director into the country. The rest of the company, including a unit manager, censor and codirector, had to be hired from the local talent pool.

The censor's job was to be sure nothing was photographed that might be in his or her eyes demeaning, debasing, or generally objectionable to the Mexican government. The Mexican codirector's mission was mainly to act as a translator.

During one such occasion I watched as Bob, directing a scene involving a Mexican actor, took the codirector aside and spoke to him briefly. What followed was a five-minute discourse in Spanish between the codirector and the actor. Later I asked Bob what he had said. With his sardonic chuckle he said, "I just asked him to tell the guy to smile more."

An hour after I joined Bob and Luther, waiting on the rock for the crew to arrive so they could start *making* this picture, the jeep returned bearing one passenger, a solemn-faced young lady dressed in somber-colored garments, carrying a black briefcase—the censor! Just what we needed: a censor—with nothing to censor.

Bob's shoulders shook with a sight and sound that was to become increasingly familiar to all of us during our Mexican stay—his suppressed ironic laughter. Perhaps this was his safety valve. Such corrosive tension, brought on by frustration and held inside, can lead to ulcers, strokes and heart attacks, and Bob would have his share of tension during his climb to the top of his profession.

Eventually, advancing like skirmishers through the thicket below us came the crew carrying pieces of equipment and chattering as they came. Finally, the actors followed.

At last, sites were selected, shots were set up, scenes were rehearsed and shot, a picture got made, and we all returned safely to California, and life went on—but what I will always remember about the land of *mañana* is how close death is to life. Not only on the highways, but on two occasions shooting the picture.

The first was when they gave me spurs with needle-sharp, three-inch rowels and a half-broke horse with crazy eyes and a personality that suggested he had been grazing on cactus.

They had "through an oversight" provided no ride-double for me, so in one shot I had to do a fast ride along the edge of a lofty precipice. While doing it, I carried one thought in my mind: One wrong, accidental touch of those spurs and I am over the side, very dead.

On the second occasion, the scene called for me, on the command "Action," to run in, duck behind a log, stay there while three shots hit the log, raise my head to look, and then exit fast.

In Hollywood, to simulate bullet hits, the special effects department drills small holes wherever needed, implants small explosive charges or squibs connected with fine concealed wire to a control panel, and, on cue, detonates them.

Another way is to have a good marksman with a compressed-air rifle stand by the camera and shoot harm-lessly disintegrating chalk bullets just where you desire them. When I saw a man with a rifle standing by the cam-era, I figured that's the way they were going to do it.

Just before the take, Bob cautioned me twice, with a very serious face, that on his command of "Action" to get in *fast* and be *sure* not to show my face until I had heard three shots and his command "GO!" Then get out fast toward a tree nearby, and *"keep on going."*

I said I understood, but I didn't really—until I heard the solid rounds smack into the log, inches from my head! The son of a bitch was shooting *live .30-.30 ammunition!*

Needless to say, on Bob's "GO!"—I went—with more live rounds tearing bark off the tree, hard on my heels.

We always had drinks and a postmortem, fortunately not my own, in Bob's suite at the hotel after each day's shooting.

On this particular day, we had a drop-in guest, a

bearded American writer everyone in the room, except me, seemed to know, who was presently living in Mexico City. Through an agent, he was selling his scripts in Hollywood under an assumed name. That's what you did in those days, when you were blacklisted, because of differences with the House Un-American Activities Committee.

The writer told a startling story, which augmented my collection of observations about life and death below the border.

"If you ever want to get rid of someone," he said, "just buy him a ticket to Mexico City. Then, for the payment of $600 to a designated police lieutenant," whose name the speaker said he could supply, "the party would be terminated." And for an extra fifty bucks the cop would get rid of the body for you.

I have not been able to verify this story, but over the years I have been leery of accepting free transportation to Mexico City.

Robert Aldrich, a generous gentleman and one of the highly respected and talented past Wizards of Hollywood, has long since flown "over the rainbow," but while he was still among us every Halloween he used to receive a wire or cablegram wishing him a Happy Halloween—signed "The Ripplehissians."

I wonder if he ever suspected they were from me.

EPILOGUE

For people who ask me, "When are you going to do another series?" I have this answer: After performing in several series, most of which are still playing worldwide, I can truthfully say, I've *done* that. What else is new?

What is so old for me that it seems new is the stage. At the Ahmanson Theatre recently, I played an ex-President in *The Best Man* (pictured earlier) with Mel Ferrer and received the best reviews of my life.

In personal appearances, actually vaudeville, I always wanted to be able to do an hour on the stage alone. I did that recently at the Roy Clark Celebrity Theatre in Branson, Missouri—the hot "new Nashville." Live theater is where I began. Live audiences excite me and bring out my best. So what is more natural than to court again my first love—live audiences?

THERAPEUTIC ACTIVITY.

Having tripped to Oz and met the "Wizards," now with my own Dorothy I am gravitating back to the place that was first *home* for me. (As the *famous* Dorothy said, there's just no place like it.)

I wanted to tell this story for the millions of young men and women—and the grownups, too—who start out bravely every morning prepared to sell something, whatever it may be. I wanted them to know the story of someone, like themselves, who has been confronted by negative people who are secure behind polished desks, and who listen doubtfully as your pitch flops.

So what do you do then? Ring up "no sale" and walk out of the office defeated? Never! Refuse to accept it! Just call it a temporary postponement of success. The difference between success and failure is often no wider than the thickness of a cigarette paper.

Just as Dorothy, the Scarecrow, the Cowardly Lion, and the Tin Woodman stood up to the Wizard and won—*so can you!*

Life's a brand-new ball game every day!

Remember that of all the elements that comprise a human being, the most important, the most essential, the one that will sustain, transcend, overcome and vanquish all obstacles is—Spirit!

"EAT YOUR HEART OUT, BILL CLINTON!"
AS JED "ZOOT" CLAMPETT GOES WITH THE FLOW.

ILLUSTRATION CREDITS

All illustrations not otherwise credited
are from the collection of the author.

MGM, 1936, Photo by Ted Allen, Pages 5, 16

Courtesy of the Historical Society, Palm Beach County,
Page 43

**Courtesy of the Henry M. Flagler Museum, Palm Beach,
Florida,** Page 44

Orange County Historical Society Inc., Page 46

Courtesy of The Bettmann Archive, New York, NY
Pages 50, 92

**Courtesy of the Rogers and Hammerstein
Organization,** Page 68

Courtesy of Stephen Cox, Pages 62, 107, 208, 220, 221,
230, 231, 232, 233, 234, 239, 247, 266

The Eric Daily Collection, Pages 144, 145, 146

Reprinted with permission from TV Guide® Magazine.
© **1978 by News America Publications Inc.,**
Page 194

© **1977 CBS, Photo by Gabi Rona. Courtesy of Motion
Picture & Television Photo Archive,**
Page 244

© **The Walt Disney Company,** Pages 198, 200, 201, 203

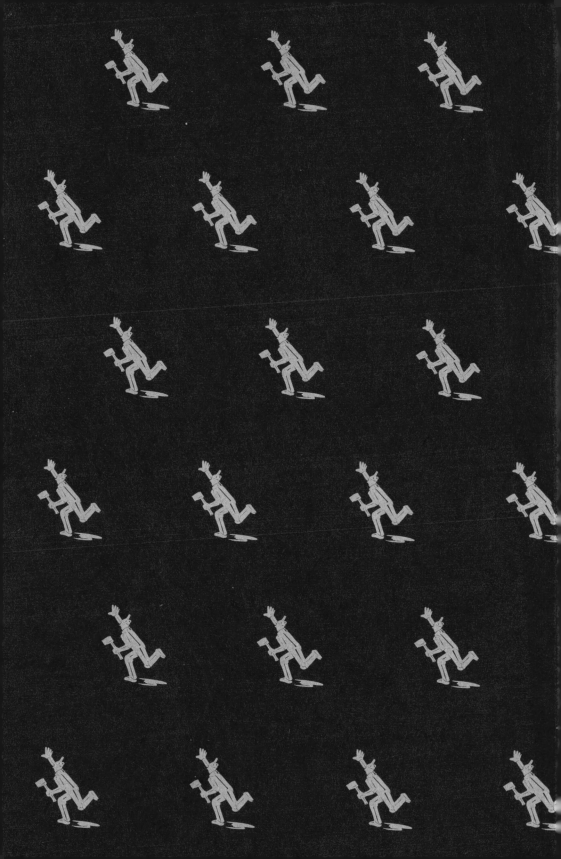